How does one begin to tell why they believe in God, a God, any God for that matter...

The concept of God does not even exist for many people and for those that do believe, He comes in many types and capabilities. Our idea of God comes from many sources. Some from family, some from culture, some from friends, just to name a few. What we believe about God depends on our source, and whether or not we believe that source to be credible. I believe. And I feel compelled to put down on paper why. If only one lost soul benefits from my effort it will be well worth my time. I suspect many will think me crazy, but God and I know the truth and that's plenty good enough for me. Let's begin.

My journey to faith in God has been a twisted tumultuous road filled with many potholes. But I am sure of my sources and thus, sure of my God, and my reasons for believing that Jesus is who He said He was. I have had doubts along the way and questioned the Bible and its integrity. But through it all I have come to know a presence within my heart and soul that comforts me, speaks to me, guides me and never leaves me. I am never alone, even when alone.

And so, I begin this written journey to convey to anyone who will see, hear, or listen, to the experiences that have led me to this profound belief in a most wonder Father, Lord, savior, and Friend. It will require that you know a bit about me to see why I have arrived at the deep faith I have in God. Keep in mind as I tell about myself that this is not an autobiography. It is a condensed story of my life so that the reader may better understand who I am and why I believe what I believe. There were many twists and turns not reveled here, but hopefully I'll present enough information to help you decide if I am a credible witness for Christ or maybe just another crackpot who got lost in the dark.

Chapter 1

My mother found herself pregnant without a husband in 1945. Not a good time in our society to be in this situation. No one would think anything about that now, but back then it was a no no. She persuaded a young man who admired her greatly to marry her and give her and me a name and a bit of respect. I carry his name to this day, but he was not my father. Of course, this union was bound to fail, and it did. Mom and I moved on.

My earliest memories are of mom and me having fun. She would ride me on her bicycle, and I felt like a little king. She would tell me how great I was and how much she loved me, and it was wonderful. I was her guy! She was my gal! Life was good. But all good things come to an end, and my world crashed and burned when my mom remarried. At age five I entered nine years of soul crushing hell.

Mom married a truck driver who drank a fair amount. I do not know the details of their relationship, but I know mom changed drastically. She went from "my gal" to a crazy person who screamed a lot and began to severely punish me for even the slightest infraction of any of her "rules". She grew worse over time and began to take pills to calm down. At first the punishments were nonviolent but still painful. She would put me on my knees on rice and make me keep my nose in a circle on the wall. At first it was a thirty minute punishment, but ten minutes was added every time I moved my nose. But over time she became violent and began to beat me, not spank, beat. It got worse over time as she had more children, and she was abusive to all of us. I got the worst of it because I would often get between my younger siblings and her. I was afraid she would severely hurt them or possibly kill them. These abuses consisted of slapping, hitting with her fists, hitting with any object at hand, dragging us through the house by our hair and ramming our head into door jams, furniture, etc.

Once started, the beating would continue till she was exhausted. It was not unusual for her attack to last 30 minutes or more. Many times, she would render us almost unconscious. She would then take a handful of pills and pass out for a while. This was not an occasional occurrence, but a daily way of life for me and my siblings. When questioned by the school about the many body bruises, she told them that neighborhood gangs were constantly attacking us on our way home. There were no buses, we walked to and home from school. As we got older, we lived in constant fear that she would eventually kill one of us and I was certain it was going to be me because of my constant interference when she was hurting one of the younger children.

    My younger brothers, Dale, and David, age 7&9 (I was 13) talked about killing her and going to reform school. We felt like we would be safer there and if she was gone the younger girls would be safe. But this didn't happen because I ran away from home (we were living in St. Louis, Mo.) May 10th, 1960, just 12 days past my 14th birthday, and went to live with my grandfather on his 'farm' in Ponchatoula, Louisiana. Of course, this didn't last. Unknown to me my grandfather had only rented the house and land and he left me alone as soon as the current crop was harvested.

    I suddenly found myself alone and on the streets and getting by as best I could. I didn't see my mom or siblings for several years. I later learned that all my siblings left home in their teens as soon as they were able to take care of themselves or found a safe haven. Many years later I got a call telling me mom had died. My brother Dale was with me and when I told him he shrugged and said "good, about time". He asked me how I felt about it. Considering the childhood abuse, I had always hated her, and yet I was sad for the loss of what should have been. Dale told me to write down how I really felt, and then burn it and I would be free. I wasn't sure that was true, in fact it seemed quite absurd. But as I pondered on all the bad memories and nightmares, I took pen in hand and began to write......

An Adult Child's Dream

30 lashes oh what a joy, the pain endured by a wee small boy.
They must think he enjoys the pain,
why else would they do it again and again?
They say they love him, can it be so?
Then why do they abuse him and torture his soul?
Why did they bring him forth on the earth?
And then rob him so completely of dignity and worth?
Were they so sick, or just plain mad,
to torture so this wee little Lad?
There was no love, no kindness, no happiness there,
Just pain and suffering and sorrow and despair.

The tortured body, the anguished soul, the loss of my
Childhood soon took it toll.
A mind full of anger, a heart turned to stone,
Unable to love, and always alone.
I suddenly awoke, with sweat on my brow,
Foolish I guess since they can't hurt me now
But as I sat in the dark, I cried for the boy
Who endured 30 lashes, oh what a joy.

    Of course, it goes without saying that burning this did absolutely nothing to abate the anger, the pain, and sorrowful memories of my childhood. Of course, the tortured body healed and has done well. But the anguished Soul, the mind full of anger, and the heart turned to stone did much to wreck my life going forward. I was unable to love even though I searched for it, and I was always alone no matter how many were around me. It was going to take something greater than me to fix me. It hurts my heart to think about the countless people who are struggling today because of a childhood filled with insanity. It is my sincere hope that my literary effort will reach out and help some of those who are trapped in the abyss of their pain and suffering.

Chapter 2

When I woke up and found my grandfather gone, I went looking for him. A neighbor informed me of his departure. I didn't know what to do, but being abandoned with no money was a far better circumstance than the one I had left. I went into the field and picked several pallets of strawberries, called a cab, took them to the feed store in town and sold them for 20 dollars. I stood on the street corner by the feed store, looked at that twenty and said, "it's just you and me", and my life on my own began. And begin it did, but not quite the blissful existence I wanted. I tried staying with several different relatives, but they were not prepared to deal with a seriously emotionally damaged 14 year old.

I tried to stay with my grandmother but didn't do well with her husband. They sent me to stay with a cousin who had a small farm. I did better there because I had animals for friends. I stayed with them for almost a year, but they had family issues and I had to go. I went to Rockford, a city west of Chicago. I knew a lady there, Mrs. Hughes, who had helped my mother when I was younger. I went to her and she graciously took me in. It was a good time. She took me to church, helped me get decent clothes and made me bathe. But I had issues and rebelled against almost everything. I didn't stay with Mrs. Hughes all the time. I hung out in various places and with questionable people, and slept in an old, abandoned car till the cops told me I needed to find another place to stay. I felt the need to head south. I went back to the farm, but they were having issues, so they took me to another cousin, Charles Bollinger, who took me in. They seemed like a happy normal family with four children. Charley was a carpenter/contractor. I really enjoyed being with them. They treated me like one of the family, took me to church, and eventually gave me job.

But all good things come to an end. My time with them was great but as in all families, conflicts arise and I had to move on. Back to bumming around and getting nowhere. But I did meet my first wife at church while staying with Charles and family. I looked her up and long story short, we wound up married. Two young fools lost in a sea of confusion guided by wounded adults who were also drowning. I was living with her mom and dad when my world dramatically changed. Keep in mind this is an overview of my life and not a detailed autobiography. We will look at my life in general, and then go back and fill in some details. Many things happened to me from the time I left mom and siblings till age twenty that are not revealed here. Most of them are not good. Life is tough for children adrift on their own.

Chapter 3

March 1966, I got a letter directing me to call the army at the number in the letter. Not sure what it was all about, I took the letter to the recruiting office in Covington, LA and asked the lady what it meant. She smiled and said I was in the army. I was supposed to contact them and they would instruct me as to where to go and what to do. I told her I didn't want to be in the army. She then asked me if I was interested in any other branch of service. I told her I didn't want to be in any type of military. Too bad she said, they will come get you if you don't call them. She asked what type of work I was doing, and I told her I was working offshore as a diver/tender. She said I could go into the navy, but I would have to decide right then as I had no choice about the army. I agreed and she signed me up in the Navy and sent me the next day for a physical in New Orleans. The following morning I was on a plane to Great Lakes naval training center. Boot Camp! I was entering a new world very different from anything I had ever experienced. And yes, they did come to the house looking for me, but I was already in the Navy. And I loved it. (Most of the time).

You would think putting a runaway street kid into a highly structured environment where he had absolutely no control would be stressful, but it was not. Free food, free bed, free money! What more could one possibly ask for! Oh, I know they tried to act tough, screamed a lot and knocked you around a little, but I found it amusing considering I had been screamed at and beaten by the toughest mom the world had to offer! Compared to her these guys were a joke. I enjoyed the military for the next twenty-nine years and seven months. A little over four years active duty and the rest in the reserves.

  The navy changed me. I was around all kinds of people with varying backgrounds. Not everyone was like me, and I liked that. Let me say up front that my military career was easy. I am not a hero. I was never in any danger. I did nothing spectacular. The closest I came to war, or any danger was desert storm. Spent 2 months on the USS COMFORT, a hospital ship. The only danger was mines in the water and possibly cruise missiles. But I came home safe and sound. I went to hospital corps school right out of boot camp, and then to Pensacola Florida naval air station hospital. While there I went to aviation med school and became a SAR (search & rescue) corpsman. Thats not as impressive as it may sound. I mostly did flight physicals for pilots and flew around in helicopters as an air-crewman. The rest of my active duty was equally unimpressive. After Pensacola I went to Kingsville Texas NAS for a year and then to Kaneohe marine corps air station in Hawaii. I might add that I love marines. From there to NAS New Orleans. I was discharged from active duty in June 1970 and transferred to the active reserves. Let me note here that I only completed the 8th grade, was in the 9th grade when I left home. I was told I probably would not advance to more than E3 without a high school diploma. While in Hawaii, I went to a local high school which offered a GED. I took a test, passed and they gave me a GED. You might be inclined to say, "oh you really do have a high school diploma". I do not. I passed a test. I got a piece of paper. I did not go to high school. Anyhow, while on active duty I had advanced to E5 and had passed the test for E6. I was told I could have the E6 if I stayed in the reserves. This is why I stayed instead of leaving completely. It proved to be a good decision. I became a commissioned officer several years later and retired as an O-4 with 29 years' service. Go figure! I never expected to get past E-3.

Life after active duty was not my idea of living. No free food, no free bed, no free money. I had no marketable skills to speak of. My military school and training meant nothing without the proper licensing required by the medical establishment. But I contacted my cousin, the contractor, and he was kind enough to provide me with a job. It was this job that brought me in contact with a man who probably changed my life without realizing it. We were building chicken houses on his property, and I assumed he was rich because of his home and land. I approached him one day and, being a bit forward, I asked him if he earned his money or inherited it. I asked if there was a secret to his success. He laughed and said he was an engineer and he had earned his money through education, hard work, and wise investments. He was facing me and suddenly he reached over and tapped me on the forehead with his finger and said, "Young man, you need to put something in there that people will pay for. That's the secret". Neither he nor I realized it then, but a seed had been planted. But God knew. I'm guessing it was part of his plan for my life.

Chapter 4

A few weeks later I found myself on a roof at Southeastern Louisiana State University. I had taken a job with a company that did tar and gravel roofing. We were redoing the roof on this building, and it was hot, and I was filthy. I could not believe I had taken a job like this. But I noticed that periodically bells would ring and all these young well-dressed folks would stream out of one building and go into another. I especially noticed the women. They were young and pretty and walking and talking with well-dressed men. It suddenly dawned on me that young ladies of their caliber would never be interested in a rag-tag uneducated street rat like me. I had come a long way in the navy, but I was still a bit crude in my speech and attitudes. And, at that moment, I was filthy and smelled bad! I had a sudden desire to be more like the young men I was observing than to be me. I was still married and not wish to leave my wife for one these women, but just had a desire to rise above my circumstances. To leave the insanity of my past and enter a world that had always seemed beyond my reach. The world of the engineer. And suddenly I remembered him tapping me on the forehead. "Put something in there that people will pay for" ... Wow! I was standing on the roof of a building that offered a way to do that. I was so excited for a moment I almost forgot I was at work and had a job to do. I didn't see Gods plan unfolding, but I think it was.

I know it was crazy, but on my lunch break I went to the admissions office. Filthy, covered with sweat and tar dust, emitting a less than desirable odor, I boldly walked up to the desk and asked what I had to do to go to their school. They initially acted like I had leprosy, but they quickly regained their composure and told me what I needed to do. And I needed to do it quickly as this was mid-August and the next semester started in September. How I pulled it off isn't important, (can you believe I passed the entrance exam!) just know I started college that September. And I entered a whole new world. It was a world full of hopes, dreams and goals. But I didn't see it that way at first. Rather than seeing it as a way to get ahead, it was my way to distance myself from my past. No one knew how screwed up my life had been. Here I was treated like a real human being. It was great.

I started that September without having a clue what I was going to major in. I met with an advisor who wanted to know what I had been doing the past few years as I was obviously older than most who enter college. He suggested I should be interested in going to medical school because of my medical experience in the navy. Sure, why not, and into the premed curriculum I went. All was good the first year. 4 A's and 1 C my first semester. Only C I made in college. But the second year they said I had to take Russian or German. I wanted to take Spanish. They said no. I was frustrated and discussed it with the doctors in my reserve unit. They told me to change my major to Nursing and Carry a chemistry and biology minor which would get me into medical school if I wanted to go. I did so and graduated with honors 3 years later.

    Getting into medical school in the 1970's was difficult. I had the grades, but I was too old or so I was told. But a friend who got in said he had 3 guys in his class that were almost 40! I called the school (LSU) and asked about this and was told these were people with advanced degrees. One of them was a CRNA. I was currently working in surgery with a heart team and was familiar with CRNA's. One of them told me there was a great school in Mobile, Alabama. New plan: go to anesthesia school and then to medical school. I applied and was accepted. Off I went on a new adventure.

Anesthesia was insane! The way I was accepted was interesting. The morning of my interview I showed up promptly at 0800 as instructed. It was pouring rain and a lot of the streets were flooded. Dr. Box, the school director, was amazed I had gotten there because half of her staff had called saying they couldn't get in through the flooded streets. When she asked me about how I was able to get there, I simply said "you told me to be here at 0800, and I'm here". She turned to the secretary and said we'll take him, he's dependable and walked off. The secretary took me to the cafeteria and got me breakfast. I wasn't quite sure what was happening and asked about the interview. She told me I already had my interview and was accepted. Let that sink in for a moment. It pays to be on time!

Most anesthesia programs are University based, but the program at USA medical center was a private school owned and run by Doctors Johnson and Box, both anesthesiologists. Their style of teaching was different, but highly effective. You learned by doing supplemented with a little instruction. It was scary at first, but we quickly became highly proficient at putting people to sleep. My first day in school I thought I was just being shown around. But no, I was put in a room with an advanced student and told WE were going to put the patient asleep. I told him I was there to watch and didn't know the first thing about putting a person to sleep. He laughed and said that it didn't matter, he would help me. WE did put the patient to sleep. The staff checked on us occasionally and the patient did quite well. The senior student obviously knew what he was doing. Within 30 days I had done 20 cases with the help of a senior student and staff, and after that I was doing cases with no help and minimal supervision. Our day would start at 6 AM. We had class for an hour, then off we went to the OR to do cases. We did this almost every day for two years. We had an occasional weekend off, and one week in the middle of each year. We averaged 60-70 hours a week. And then, suddenly, it was over. I graduated and started working. I assure you this is a very brief description of my anesthesia training. It was an interesting and stressful moment in my life. I spent the next 40 plus years putting folks to sleep. (And waking them up!)

Chapter 5

Fresh out of school I went to work for Dr. Johnson. As a senior he had asked me to stay at the medical center and do cases and help with the anesthesia students. I agreed and worked for a little over a year before leaving. From there I went to work for Anesthesia services at the Mobile Infirmary in Mobile, AL. I left there in august 1987 and quit doing anesthesia for a year. I was burned out. Too many cases, too many hours spent in the hospital, and too tired of working with doctors who thought they were better than everyone else. What did I do for the next year you ask?

I had gotten involved with an insurance company, AL Williams, which I am sure many of you have heard of. I was doing this on the side while doing anesthesia. I became exposed to a whole new financial concept that could possibly insulate me even farther from my past. I learned about all kinds of insurance, but even better, I learned about the stock market. I also learned about real estate and began to buy rental properties. Long story short, I got licensed for life insurance, and securities. I was able to show folks a better way to save and to protect their families. I loved doing this and I was beginning to hate anesthesia due to the unnecessary stress put on us by the circumstances I had to work in. I had begun to make a little money doing this and I reasoned that I could be very successful if I did it full time. So you see, a no brainer, trade what I didn't like for what I loved doing. I had some money saved and saw no problem.

      This year in the insurance and securities business taught me more about human beings than I had learned in my entire life to date. I learned more about greed, lying, Cheating, family ties, stupidity, willful ignorance, back-stabbing, and dishonesty than I really cared to know. And these are the good folks. I was surer of the people in the streets than I was of the many different types of people I encountered in the financial industry. Let me take this opportunity to help you financially. No one will manage your assets with a purer motive than you will. You need to read some books on insurance and investing, and learn how to manage your money, or at least learn enough to know when the people who are doing it for you are blowing smoke up your??? You must be able to identify when they are being dishonest with you. Do not trust them just because you are friends or a relative. Educate yourself!! The Bible says we perish from a lack of knowledge. And nowhere is this more true than in the financial world. Enough said. I have cleared my conscience where you are financially concerned.

I learned a lot about myself from this experience. Despite my past and many character flaws, I discovered that I am basically an honest person. While I have done many deeds I am not proud of (just like you), I found it hard to lie to people just to secure a higher commission for me than to do what was best for them. I also felt compassion for the "little" people. You know, the ones no one cares about. The ignorant masses that are there to be sheared like sheep. The ones we use to line our pockets while they suffer the results of our greed and dishonesty. Once again, I began to feel the pain of hating what I had become a part of. I was barely able to make enough to live on by being honest. Or maybe I was just no good at what I was doing. I also learned the rental business was the dumbest thing I had tried to do. What was I thinking! I began to think maybe anesthesia was a better choice for me. I didn't want to work for the local folks, so I called a temp service and started doing temporary anesthesia gigs. And strangely enough, I enjoyed it. But always on the road and living in hotels is not as glamorous as it sounds so I soon tired of this too. Keep in mind this is an overview of my life, not a detailed autobiography. There were other things going on in my life that caused me pain and distress. I will address them later.

    I had been working as a locum (temp worker) for several months when I got a call one morning from Knollwood Hospital in Mobile. Their anesthesia group didn't show up. They had quit without notice. One of the surgeons, Dr Zarzour, had surgery scheduled and had no one to put his patient to sleep. He told them to call me and see if I would come. They did and I did. Thus began my employment at Knollwood Park Hospital. It was a great job. Close to home and hassle free. The hospital hired another CRNA and an anesthesiologist. We worked well together and for a time I was quite content with my job. This lasted a little over a year till USA Medical Center took over Knollwood in mid to late 1990. I initially left for a few weeks, but the med center asked me to stay at Knollwood, and I accepted. A few weeks later I was called up and sent to the Middle East for Desert Storm. I returned to Knollwood two months later and stayed until the Mobile Infirmary took over Knollwood Hospital. I then went to the USA Medical Center main OR where I have been till now, 2023, age 77.

Chapter 6

Well now you might say to yourself, it sounds like you did quite well for yourself. Maybe you had a bit of a rough start but look where you wound up. Sounds good, huh? Well, I left out the parts about the 4 wives, the drug and alcohol addiction, bad decisions, incredible debt, my five children and the seething anger I could never seem to get rid of. Factor these things in and we go from utopia to hades rather quickly. Of course, these things didn't take place separately, they were all entwined in one long nightmare with moments of fun and fantasy making the journey difficult to escape from. But let's take these things one at a time and see if you really think my life was as successful as it may appear to be.

I guess I'll begin with the drinking and drugging as this was a significant part of my life and probably a cause of many of the destroyed relationships that I had entered hoping to find that love and happiness that I had never had. It also contributed significantly to stupid decisions made in moments of stupor which proved to be incredibly disastrous and costly.

I never drank or took drugs in any form til I was 19 years old. I was working offshore in Louisiana when the journey started. After our two weeks offshore, the guys would pile in their vehicles and head for home. Problem was…. They stopped at every bar along the way. Now I was just a young skinny kid who looked out of place with all these redneck bubbas who worked offshore. And they made sure to harass me and tell me how pretty I was. But that began to change once I started drinking with them. Once I got a few rounds in me I changed. I suddenly wasn't scared anymore. My anger subsided and I felt wonderful.

I also noticed something strange considering drinking was new for me. I could drink more than the rednecks before I became drunk. Over time I became known for the large amount of liquor I could consume and still be standing. At parties friends would secretly keep putting booze in my glass every time I sat it down. I didn't realize how much I was drinking because my glass was always at least half full!!! But this all changed when I went into the Navy. Oddly enough, I quit drinking for three years.

I know you want to know what the difference was considering what great boozers sailors can be. This may sound corny, but I really was into being the best I could be. I also had a son while stationed in Hawaii and was really getting in to being a father. When I had only a few months left on active duty, my wife returned home early so I was alone there the last few months before getting off active duty. Wow!! Guess what I discovered living in the barracks? Weed!!!!! I had never done any drugs and was not drinking much at the time. But the guys turned me onto the best high I ever had. I stayed stoned most of time when not on duty. But this ended too when I went to NAS New Orleans for discharge.

As noted previously, I did a couple of jobs after discharge and wound up in college. It was the 70's and you just had to be there to understand. I was doing well academically, but my personal life was descending into hades. My wife (first one) didn't want me to go to college. She wanted me to get a job and buy her a house. I told her these things would come in time, but she wanted them now! I know it was rough for her, but I went to class all day, worked at the hospital at night, and worked for my cousin 12 hours Saturday and Sunday. I had to do this to pay for school and take care of her. I assure you, it was tough on me too! It's not easy to get by on 4 hrs of sleep but is not that difficult if you smoke enough of the right stuff. I didn't want to get busted for drugs and end my possible future medical career, so I grew my own weed to avoid cops and dealers. I had also dabbled in a variety of substances (speed, mushroom tea, quaaludes, and some offered that I still do not know what they were) but, after graduating college I pretty much stopped doing drugs and stuck mostly to alcohol which was legal and did not endanger my nursing license. I believe that going into a profession which required a license saved my life because I really enjoyed drugs.

Had I stayed in construction or some area that did not require drug testing I would have been completely lost. While consuming large quantities of alcohol is not good, I still believe God saved me by starting me on a path that got me to where I am today. But the drinking took me down a path I didn't need or want to go. "Sin has a way of taking you farther than you meant to go, keeping you there longer than you meant to stay, and costing you way more than you meant to pay." I didn't come up with this interesting saying, but I have found it to be oh so true in my life.

    Going to Anesthesia school was a wise decision, but there was a powerful incentive in the 70s to drink, party, and just be stupid in general. Many of the students in the school were heavy drinkers and on the weekends that we did have off we partied hard. We were cold sober in school, but on our time we did our best to stay in La La Land! After anesthesia school the drinking continued for a while, but something happened that caused me to stop. A friend talked to me about God and invited me to church. We began going on a regular basis and our lives began to change in several ways. I quit drinking, cussing and began to experience a peace and calm that was most welcome. This lasted for a couple of years and life was good. Enter stupid. I think I challenged satan and he didn't like it. During a conversation with my pastor and another church member about how lucky we were to have freedom to worship and had bibles readily available, I foolishly said I knew enough scripture, and was a strong enough Christian that I could take whatever the devil threw my way. How stupid of me. I slowly began to slip back into my old way of living. It didn't help that my wife (second one) enjoyed drinking and had never stopped like I did.

  We became involved with groups and people who also drank a lot and had neighbors who drank a lot. So, it became a way of life to just get up, go to work, come home and sit around and drink all evening with friends. I also wound up on occasion being in the wrong crowd and taking God knows what. Obviously by this time God and church was in the rear-view mirror. Looking back, I can see I was just playing church. And despite significant experiences that made me know God was real, it just didn't reach deep enough into my soul to keep me on the straight and narrow. I guess I just hadn't reached bottom yet. Lots of people were doing lots of drugs and liquor in those days. (And still do). It goes without saying that long hours of work and endless drinking soon took a toll on my family. I soon found myself divorced and alone. But it was ok, I had drinking and drugging buddies and an open highway to the wine, women, and song that I thought was the answer to the ever-brewing storm that raged inside me.

      I was single, I was free, I was young and handsome and the deceiver in me convinced me I was the cat's meow!!! I had raised stupid to an art form. I had always told myself I could quit anytime and would do so when I found the perfect woman, the perfect job and was in total control of my destiny. I know the Bible says to not call anyone a fool, but I must point out that I was, indeed, a fool at this phase of my life. It didn't matter how much wine, how many women, or many songs, the lonely empty little boy inside could not seem to pull it together and escape the insanity of my youth. "The tortured body, the anguished soul, the loss of my childhood soon took its toll. A mind full of anger, a heart turned to stone, unable to love and always alone." Desperately clawing my way through life wasn't working. Something had to give. And it did.

  Caring people around me began to see something was terribly wrong and reached out to me. I initially rejected them as I was certain I had everything under control. But in time even the great James Portier had to admit he was in trouble and needed help to survive. Fortunately, the board of nursing had a program for addicted nurses who self-reported that would allow them to keep their license and enter treatment. And my employer had a program for nurses to return to work after completing recommended treatment. I made the first wise decision in a long time and took advantage of both programs.

Chapter 7

I entered Talbott Recovery Center in Atlanta, GA. In Oct 1996. I didn't know what to expect. I knew I was out of control in some areas of my life and needed some help. But I still didn't realize I had a problem with alcohol. After all, how many folks do you know that can drink a fifth of whiskey every day or more, and still function normally? In my mind I thought I was going to learn how to drink moderately, responsibly. It took six weeks for me to realize I was an alcoholic/addict and had no control over my life or alcohol (or occasional drugs). I had been there about eight weeks when a counselor encountered me in the hallway talking to myself. He gently put his hand on my shoulder, looked me straight in the eyes, and gently said "jimmy, you need to let go and let God fix you or you will never be free." It was a defining moment in my life. I had several opinions about God and not all of them good. But I had begun to respect the treatment center and the counselors and pay attention to what they said. After all, all of them had once been addicted and screwed up like me. And I desperately wanted to be less like me and more like them.

I went out behind the building and sat down by a pine tree. I looked at it and recalled the Bible said that Jesus had made all things. If that is so, then He made the pine tree. The very fact the tree existed proved there was a tree maker. So I began to talk to the maker of the pine tree. I couldn't see Him, but I certainly could see and feel the tree He had made. So I simply said to Him that I wasn't sure if He existed or not, but I needed help. That my way of living wasn't working, but if He would help me I was willing to let go and let Him control my life. It's hard to explain what happened from this point on, but something was different, something in me started changing. The next day I sat and pondered where I was and all that my life had been. What was the reason for all the insanity? Why do we let ourselves get so messed up? And suddenly I came to the realization that I was not totally responsible for my situation. There was something going on besides my stupidity. The Bible says satan goes about seeking those he can destroy. I certainly didn't start out as a child to be unhappy and screw up my life. Could it be I have viciously been deceived? Tricked into a way of thinking that was designed to destroy me? I took pen in hand and began to write what I thought had happened and where I might find the answer to a better life.   I wrote:

The Deceiver

There is a deceiver, I deal with him every day

He tries to direct my every thought, and influence what I say.

He's like an unseen hand that tries to control my entire life,

And he seems to thrive on misery & pain & suffering & strife!

He chips away at all thats good til there's almost nothing left to save,

Til you're all alone, your life is gone, and you've become his total slave!

What manner of deceiver is this that I have come to know,

Who has so completely eaten away the fabric of my life,

And now seeks to consume my soul!

Will I ever escape, will I ever get free? Is there not any hope for me?

Or will I lose it all, and to continue to fall into the abyss of the deceived?

I think not, I will not!!

For despite my fall I'm not lost at all,

Because God reaches out His Hand to me!!!!!!

And reach out to me He did. My thinking changed. I began to feel a sense of hope that I had never experienced. I began to look around and see other lost souls desperately trying to make sense of their insane existence and realized I was not alone but was one of millions who were just like me. And suddenly I knew, not sure how, but knew that God was the answer. I began reading my Bible, talking to the pine tree maker, and doing what my counselor told me. The result was remarkable.

The intense anger, the frustration with life that had haunted me my entire life began to melt away and I got a sense of calm and peace that was truly amazing. And suddenly I realized God was giving me a second chance to get it right. Not like before, but really right this time. And He brought to my memory past experiences that I had had to help me know He was real and still looking out for me. The Bible says that when God controls your life there is a peace that defies all understanding. I can absolutely confirm this. Remember, I am still in drunken junkie camp, my life is still in shambles, my future uncertain, but it was OK! I somehow knew life was going to get better because I was getting better thanks to the pine tree Maker. For those who don't know who the pine tree Maker is, He was the one on the cross in the middle.

After 18 weeks they decided I had recovered enough to go home. I must admit I was a bit apprehensive at the thought of going back to the same environment without the option of chemical backup. But it wasn't at all what I expected. I thought everybody would look down on me for having a "problem". I expected to be behind with all my bills. Money was a concern as I had not worked in over 4 months. What was amazing and makes me believe more strongly in God's grace and mercy, is that no one cared. Half my coworkers didn't even know I was gone, (not as special as I thought I was) and the other was glad I was back so they didn't have to work as much! No one cared what I had done or where I had been. And my bills? It seems I had enough vacation and sick time to cover my whole absence. It all ran out the week I came home. It was all good. (I had a friend taking care of my finances while I was gone). But the real miracle of my return was my return to work. All CRNA's who go through treatment must work as a nurse and not do anesthesia for at least a year. I was released on Saturday, signed a recovery contract with the board of nursing on Tuesday, and returned to work on Thursday doing anesthesia! This was made possible because the chief of the anesthesia department recommended it to the board of nursing and agreed to be responsible for me. I am the only CRNA in the state of Alabama to return directly to work after treatment. I shall be forever grateful to Dr. Weis for taking me under his wing and allowing me to return. It was the hand of God working on my behalf.

Chapter 8

They told us not to get into any relationship if we were single for at least a year. Get a plant. If it survived 6 months, get a pet. If that worked out we could date after a year. They wanted us to care about something besides ourselves for a while. I did one better. I stayed single for 5 years. Yes, I dilly-dallied a bit in short non-serious relationships. I did get a plant. It lived for almost 10 years! And I did way too many pets. I was always picking up strays and had close to 30 at one time. It was a strange mix of dogs and cats, and potbellied pigs. It just felt good to be surrounded by something alive that loved me.

There is not much more to my drinking/drugging story. I have stayed clean and sober since 1996. I did have a short mini relapse for lack of a better way to say it. My third wife whom I married 5 years into my recovery liked to drink and told me she had a right to do so. She wanted me to have a glass of wine with her at dinner. She bought a book called "controlled drinking for the recovered alcoholic". In a moment of stupid I agreed to give it a try. After all, I was trying to make my marriage work and it seemed so important to her. She had a drinking problem that she hid from me til we were married. It didn't take but a few weeks for me to discover that I was poking a sleeping giant within and needed to stop. Thank goodness I was attending AA meetings and had a good sponsor who immediately jerked me back to reality as soon he found what was going on. Needless to say, she would not stop drinking, and I was not able to deal with the insanity of the relationship, and we divorced.

Staying clean and sober is easy if you follow the rules for doing so. After the divorce I decided to never marry again. I went to AA meetings, attended church faithfully, read my Bible and surrounded myself with non-drinking friends. I worked and spent time with my son from the last insane marriage. Life was good again. From then till now there has been no desire to drink or involve myself with folks that do. Well now you may say, it seems like you made it just fine. Really? All you know by now is a brief life history, and my drinking/drugging history. Let me now discuss 4 marriages and the absolute stupid insanity experienced in 3 of them. And we will discuss soul crushing debt that comes with multiple trips into stupid trying to ease the pain of one's past with relationships. Of wrongly believing that a woman can fix the damage inflicted by a "woman"! And the joy and sorrow that comes with 5 children with 4 women.

Chapter 9

I have been married 4 times. I wish it wasn't so, but it is. I would have liked to marry one wonderful woman and stayed with her forever. But that was not to be. "A mind full of anger, a heart turned to stone, unable to love and always alone". This combined with copious amounts of drugs and booze is not a good recipe for a healthy lasting relationship. But I had not yet started my addiction journey when I met and married my first wife. As I discuss my wives I will try to do in a manner as truthful as I can, from my point view, without revealing anything or accusing anyone of the bad "stuff" to cause you to take one side or the other. Just know that these relationships were painful, mentally, emotionally and financially.

Round one.. I was 16 and living with the Bollinger family in Folsom, Louisiana. We went to a little country church called savannah branch church, named after a small river nearby. One Sunday morning I walked in and saw an angel sitting in the pews and she was smiling at me. It's amazing the feelings that can sweep through the heart of a love starved lad aided by an abundance of testosterone. I was smitten. I got to know her and her family, and long story short, we were married a year later. Yes, we were too young to sign the papers, but our parents stepped up and signed for us. It was a case of two young fools lost in a sea of confusion aided and abetted by adults who were wounded and drowning themselves. We were married from 1963 to 1972 and had a son while I was stationed in Hawaii in the navy. Upon discharge I had a couple of jobs, but fate led me to Southeastern Louisiana State University. She was unhappy with me going to college. She wanted me to get a job and build her a new house with my VA loan. I refused to quit school, so she divorced me. She also got full custody of our son. This happened because I didn't know she was divorcing me and didn't show up in court. I was ordered to pay for the lot and trailer we were buying, but it belonged to her per court order. It was a struggle, but I managed to get through school and pay what I owed her.

    There was much that happened during this marriage that I don't feel inclined to write about. Just know that flaws in our character created much pain and disappointment, and of course our love affair with weed and booze didn't help. We survived it, but our son paid a terrible price for our stupidity that I have deeply regretted. Immaturity, jealousy, selfishness, and booze won this round.

Round 2: I remained single for 5 years. I graduated from college and got a fantastic job in Baton Rouge Louisiana working with a group of heart surgeons. I was 29 years old, free and living the good life, or so I thought. I had a few short relationships, but just couldn't seem to find that perfect woman that I thought I needed to make my life complete. And then it happened again. I walked into the x-ray department at Baton Rouge General Hospital and guess what happened? I saw another angel. I was smitten! Long story short, we dated for 3 years and got married while I was in anesthesia school. This one lasted 10 years. She got the house and new car and a significant amount to live on. Interestingly, we didn't go to court. We sat down and drew up an agreement, gave it to our attorney and
Were divorced in 2 days. We have remained the best of friends. We just acknowledged we were not making it and simply parted ways. Of course, I remained active with our 2 children. So what happened you ask? It was the 70's. We drank a lot. Our friends drank a lot. Our neighbors drank a lot. We did for a time attend

church and everything went fine, but we got sideways in the road, too many drinking opportunities, and God just went by the wayside. My bad! And once again I have left out many bitter details which serve no purpose to reveal. Just know that 10 years and 2 children were painful. We had some good times but not nearly enough to offset the stupidity and incredible emotional pain that goes with failing relationships. Drugs, alcohol, stupidity, and selfishness won this round.

Round 3.. in 1998 I met an incredible woman via a multi-level marketing fiasco. She was bright, funny, loved animals, and really seemed to care about me. I think this was the deceiver's finest moment in my life. She lived in Illinois and I in Mobile, Alabama. After many phone sessions over many months, I decided to go visit her and find out who this lovely person was who seemed, at least in conversations, so right for me, or so I thought. I visited her several times and thought I had finally found the dream woman I had been looking for my whole life. She lived on a farm, had horses, dogs and cats. I absolutely love animals and was perhaps blinded by her situation which kept me from getting a better look at her. She eventually moved to Alabama, and we got married. I have made a number of mistakes in my life, but this one ranks very near the top of the list. The problem was…I am an alcoholic/drug addict in recovery. I cannot be around or live in an environment where any addictive substances are readily available. I should have been suspicious when I found wine in her refrigerator before I married her. But she said it was for cooking only, that she seldom ever drank, and that she would cease to drink or use it for cooking considering my history. Our problems started immediately after getting married. If you recall this was the wife who told me she had a right to drink. She got me a book on responsible drinking for recovered alcoholics because she wanted me to drink with her. She started drinking openly as soon as we were married. She would drink a 5 liter box of wine daily. I was shocked by this behavior and soon realized she had the same problem with alcohol I had. I asked her mother if she was aware of how much her daughter drank. She said she had been a heavy drinker for many years. I asked her why she didn't tell me about it before we got married. She said, "you never asked me". We also had many other issues pile up that made life for me a living hell. I liked her better drunk because then she was easier to get along with.

She also spent money like it grew on trees. And feeding and caring for the 9 horses she brought to Alabama cost me a small fortune. The constant screaming and bickering kept me so depressed I hated to go home. I would sit in my driveway and cry and beg God to just let me die rather than face her. I'm sure I was part of the problem, but most of the problems probably could have been worked out if it were not for the drinking. There were a couple of other serious issues we had, but it serves no purpose to discuss them. Suffice it to say this was an unfortunate relationship for all concerned. We divorced after 4 years. Both of us needed some relief. We also had a son and the stress was not good for him. Alcohol, selfishness, irresponsibly, stupidity and crushing debt won this round.

Chapter 10

Final round... my 3rd marriage had so crushed me mentally, emotionally, and financially that I vowed to never marry or have anything to do with a woman ever again. I would rather die than to repeat that insanity. I talked to God about it and told Him that for me to involve myself again with a woman she would need to be a faithful Christian, 5'7". Long dark hair, blue eyes, short waist, long legs, 115-125 lbs., and would have to walk up and say God sent me. She needed to be frugal, soft spoken, slow to anger, trustworthy, and love God more than me. I felt safe as we all know this woman does not exist. But if God can build a 4-lane highway to Hawaii, then this was a chip shot for him.

Don't know about the highway? Let me tell you the story. A man was afraid to fly so he asked God to build a highway to Hawaii for him. God explained that he, the man, didn't fully understand what he was asking. The long distance through the deepest ocean in the world would be a massive undertaking. God asked if there was something he needed that was much more easily accomplished. The man thought about it for a minute, then asked God to give him enough wisdom to understand his wife. God asked him if he wanted a 2 lane or 4 lane.

Why would I ask God for something I knew didn't exist? To keep me safe! There are many women who could fill some of these requirements, but no one can fill them all. Or so I thought. It seems one was already there at Life Church which I attended regularly. There was a woman that stood in the back of the church for praise and worship and would sing in sign language. I really liked to watch her but gave her no thought beyond that. I spoke to her a couple of times, but she brushed me off. But one Sunday morning she walked up to me, said God sent her to give me a message which she had written on a slip of paper. She had written what I had been praying about!

I suddenly felt like my life was going to change. I carefully began to observe this woman and eventually asked her to go to lunch after church. She said she didn't date and seemed to have no interest in going anywhere with me. But I kept asking her each week and she eventually said I could come to the park and walk with her and her children. And I did. We walked and talked, and I began see her through Gods eyes, not mine. I saw a good woman who loved God, and had a very calming effect on me.

    This walk in the park went on for a few weeks and she seemed to like me. Then, suddenly, she asked me to meet her family one Sunday afternoon. They all met on a regular basis and had family time. Johanna had been divorced 10 years, had never dated, and I think her family was a bit surprised to meet me. But it was a wonderful visit for me. No drinking, cussing, arguing. Just a big family who all believed in God and acted accordingly. A real live Brady bunch. And they all seemed to like each other. My life being what it was, this seemed like a fairy tale family. Of course, they had no idea about my life and how their family affected me.

    She still would not go on a regular date, but she liked to ride in the country, and we did so. We discussed our budding relationship and agreed if it was to be, it must be done God's way. No intimacy before marriage, regular church attendance, tithing, and always being honest with one another. Did I mention she was 5'7", 117 lbs., long dark hair, blue eyes, short waist, long legs, soft spoken, frugal, and I trusted her completely.

    She never seemed to get angry and made it clear that Jesus was always going to be the most important person in her life. I asked everyone who knew her if she was for real, and everybody said she was special. She was an angel. I was divinely smitten. We met in February and got married in September. I have never regretted it. The first 2-3 years had some rough moments, but we were determined to honor our commitment to God and to each other. It took a while to learn how she needed to be treated and loved, but we eventually reached the point where we began to understand and appreciate our differences and enjoy our similarities. Blended families always have issues that need to be worked out. Considering our extreme differences in life I think we did quite well.

    Pruning is painful, but necessary for growth. I love and appreciate her more every day and cannot imagine my life without her. Commitment, and Godly living won this round.

Chapter 11

With wives come children. I have 4 boys and 1 girl. I had 1 boy with first wife, 2 boys with second wife, 1 boy with third wife, and a daughter with a woman I was not married to. I love them all. I have not discussed this book with them so I will refrain from naming them but will simply tell you about them. 2 are gay, 3 are straight. 2 believe in God. 2 are not sure about God, and 1 doesn't appear to believe in God. I have experienced the joy of young children, the insanity of teenagers, and the eventual pride that comes with them growing up and doing well. My relationship with each is different. I love them all in different ways. They are all very special to me and I am proud to be their father. I regret my addiction prevented me from being a better dad, but I did my very best to be there for them and see that they were cared for. I never had a father, so I didn't know how to be one. I just tried to do for them what I wished someone had done for me. In spite of the divorces, I always supported my children and was always there for them. My daughter didn't know I was her father until she was 30. I deeply regret this as I missed watching her grow up. She is a very special lady and I love her much. It serves no purpose to reveal more about my children, so I will stop here. Just know life has not been easy for me. Not having my children with me due to divorce and seeing the pain it caused them has not been easy. Living life God's way would certainly have been better. It is my sincere hope that they will see the change God has made in me and know that serving Him will bring the peace and contentment that we all are so desperately seeking. God's way always wins.

Chapter 12

Debt is a loser... Let's now discuss this millstone that most of us have hung around our neck at one time or the other. It's a life killer. Especially if not properly entered or managed. We all go into debt. Homes, cars, "stuff". Some of us do well, but for most it is a daily struggle to simply get by.

We all want to live great lives full of love, fun, adoration, and anything else that will hopefully fill that hole in our soul that only God can fill. But we have all bought the lie. We just need more and more to be happy. And how do we get more? Debt, more debt, unmanageable debt, and soul crushing debt. But look at how happy we are! Look at all we have! Not!!!

It's fun for a while, but when it comes time to pay the piper, we find we are unable to do so. So, then we get to experience anxiety, fear, frustration, embarrassment, depression, and a whole host of unpleasant feelings that are not easy to manage. But it's ok. We have drugs, alcohol, and improper habits and relationships to help us with these emotions and situations. Of course, this most often leads to broken homes, broken people, and broken children. The landscape of humanity is littered with the broken hopes, dreams and bodies of its victims.

  The Bible is quite clear about debt. It stresses that we should be the lender and not the borrower. We need to study Gods Word and learn the correct way to manage our money. Then we will prosper and find some of the peace and contentment we are looking for. We may not get rich by worldly standards, but God promised us enough. And enough with God is better than excess without Him.

  My affair with debt began after I got out of the navy. I borrowed to buy a piece of land and a trailer. I then started college and worked 7 days a week. It was tough, but I managed to pay for school and my mortgage and provide for a wife and child. I paid the mortgage and trailer off and it went to my wife via divorce. I next bought a house in Baton Rouge la., but I was working, and it was no strain. My next mortgage was in Mobile, AL while in anesthesia school. As soon as I graduated, I bought another house, but kept the last one, and traded the house in Baton Rouge for a duplex in Mobile. I now had a home and 2 rental properties. I went to a real estate seminar to learn more about rental properties. Guess what they said?

Debt is great. Always use other people's money to purchase property. I learned how to buy property with no money down, and I was off to the races. I had discovered the pathway to great wealth and was determined to take it. I didn't want to get rich just to be rich, but more so to insulate me from my past. Also remember I am getting deep into my drinking by this time. The alcohol was messing with my thinking, leading me down a path I didn't need to go. But everything I touched turned to gold, or so I thought.

I started buying houses, renovating them and renting them out. Repairs were costing a lot, but I was making a lot of money at the hospital and could manage. I kept buying and getting deeper and deeper into debt. But it was ok. It was other people's money, and I had renters. But somewhere around 8-10 properties the expenses began to outpace my income. And yet I kept going. And I learned something about rental property that they didn't teach at the seminar. Vacancies, appliances and a/c repairs, non-paying freeloaders and eviction nightmares. Plus, many renters destroy property. I was becoming overwhelmed. But I was drinking more and more, and the deceiver convinced me I could handle it. But I couldn't. This was happening in the eighties and hundreds of thousands in mortgage debt was a lot of money. I started moonlighting on weekends at other hospitals to get enough money to feed the beast I had created. The stress of work, debt, and constant drinking ended my second marriage. She kept the house and I paid for it.

The stress of not being with my boys plunged me into a depression that only got me to drinking more. I was free and alone. But I had to continue to work and try to manage all the properties I had acquired. I stayed on this merry go round til the early 90's. And then suddenly I couldn't do it anymore. I called a realtor friend and told him to sell all my rental properties which he did. I made enough to pay all the mortgage's but had very little left over. And then I got the shock of my life 3 years later when the IRS slapped me with a bill for approximately 35 thousand dollars.

A new lesson! All the write offs for several years of rental property insanity had to be paid back! But I had no money. Years Of foolish living and spending left me in a hole that I didn't have any way of climbing out of. I finally came to the point where I realized I needed help. I couldn't seem to quit drinking or make good decisions anymore. This was in 1996.

I took advantage of a recovery program and put the IRS on hold. Skipping forward, I incurred no new debt for five years after coming out of the recovery center and was able to pay all bills except for a mortgage on one house I still owned, and I managed to pay the IRS! While married to my third wife I built a home on 20 acres I owned. 240K mortgage. But I could handle it. I was not drinking, had a good job, and it was what my wife wanted. This was the drinking wife. 9 horses and spending 2-3 thousand a month more than I was earning put me deep in debt by the time we divorced after 4 years. I owed 90 thousand on credit cards and was paying over a thousand a month in interest. It's amazing how stupid can screw up your life. But better times were on the way.

My 4th wife was very frugal and spent very little money, she encouraged me to tithe and give God an opportunity to help me with my finances. It was slow going at first, but over 10 years I managed to pay off both mortgages and credit cards. Today I am debt free and have saved several hundred thousand dollars which is steadily growing thanks to wise investments.

There you have it. My debt history. As of this writing I am 77 years old and have been debt free for several years. Had I never drank I would have probably been way ahead financially. Investing while drunk cost me approximately 300 thousand in losses. I don't recommend options on futures unless you really know what you are doing. Obviously, I did not. Letting brokers trade my accounts was another mistake that cost me close to 75 thousand dollars. These are not large sums of money today but were huge losses back when they occurred.

Chapter 13

I guess it's time for a recap. As I have stated this is not an autobiography although it may seem like one. I have attempted to give you an overview of my life so you can make a better evaluation of who I am. Am I for real or just some kook whose writing method is confusing to say the least?

Let's see now just what I have covered. My history, my drinking history, marriage history, brief offspring history, and my debt history. I didn't go into work history too much because I have basically been doing anesthesia for the last 46 years, as of 2022. I didn't cover many details like fun trips, vacations, happy times etc. The trip to Hawaii was great, 5 cruises were fun, Disney world with the kids was both fun and tiring. We did all the things that families do in spite of the insanity of our lives. I always presented myself to the world as happy and living the dream. But the reality was very different.

So, to sum me up I am a mixed breed, Cherokee/Choctaw/German/Irish or so I was told by my grandmother and other relatives. I look like a Native American. Grew up in an abusive environment, left home at age 14 and lived in the streets or wherever I could to hang out. I have no criminal record but have spent a night or two in jail on several occasions including several days in jail in Reynosa, Mexico. I don't recommend it. Married 4 times and had several "friends". Don't recommend this either! Five children. 29 years with US navy- 4 active, 25 reserve. Alcoholic/addict in recovery 26 years. (Still addicted to food!) College graduate. CRNA. Father, husband, and grandfather to some wonderful young people thanks to my wife.

My first job was setting pins in a bowling alley. I had several jobs in construction which helped some with the rental properties. I have worked offshore as a deckhand, and later as a diver tender. It was that job that landed me in the navy. I basically odd-jobbed my way through life until college. There's more, but I think this is enough for you to get a handle on who I am.

I have no doubt I have touched on something thus far that you can well understand, have experienced, or identify with. Perhaps you or someone in your family has a similar background. I am no different than you.

As a young man I had hopes, dreams, desires. But somewhere along the way life destroyed my dream. I was drowning and needed a lifeline that no one could seem to provide. And so, we come to the purpose of this book. I found the lifeline I needed. Finding it didn't come easy but I did find it. I will try to record the many experiences which I consider to be the hand of God working in my life. I need to point out here that I have done no research for this book. No notes, no outlines.

    I simply sat down with my notebook, my memories, and began to write. I am 77 years old and pulling up a lifetime of memories takes some time. I have written this over several months as my memory has permitted. I will start with some experiences that can only be described as a miracle. Then experiences that lead me to believe that God was looking out for me. We will finish up with interesting facts that I have learned through seeking proof of God. And then final thoughts and comments. And perhaps a mention of those people who have impacted me in a profound way. So, without further ado let us begin where it began for me. Age 10. Evangelist Oral Roberts.

Chapter 14

The wart.... Around age 8 a skin lesion began to grow smack dab in the middle of my forehead! Not a big deal at first, but over a couple of years it got bigger and longer. It was about a quarter inch long and about half the size of a number 2 lead pencil. It began to embarrass me as I thought I looked like a unicorn! Mom took me to a doctor and had it removed, but it grew back bigger and longer. In addition to its unsightly appearance, it was prone to bleed profusely when manipulated. I was constantly waking up with blood in my bed from turning over in my sleep and dragging it across my pillow. It was not a fun experience for me. About that time an evangelist, Oral Roberts, had come to Rockford, Ill. where we lived and had a big tent revival. It was a big thing because the word was, he could lay his hand on you and you would be healed. And, of course, we went to several of his meetings. I personally saw people get up and walk from wheelchairs. He had a man with him who was blind in one eye and had a fake eye in the socket. He would take his fake eye out, cover his good eye, and read folks driver licenses with his empty eye socket. Many people seemed to be getting healed from a whole host of ailments. Was it all real?? I don't know. But I can tell you what I do know for a fact. Mom took me through the healing line. Mr. Roberts simply touched my forehead, and said "in the name of Jesus", and then we moved on. Nothing happened. Wart is still there. Didn't fall off. I was disappointed. So much for healing I thought. Where was God when I needed Him. But a strange thing happened as we left the meeting. There were a lot of people trying to get out of the tent exit ways, and I was pushed and fell down. As I fell my head just barely missed a stake in the ground holding the tent ropes. But not completely. The stake brushed across my forehead and sliced off my wart smoothly with my forehead. I momentarily panicked expecting blood to start pouring down my face as had happened before. But there was no blood!!! Just a red spot where the wart had been. And the next morning when I woke up the red spot was gone!!! The wart never returned. Completely gone and no scar. You may not believe Oral Roberts could heal or help anyone, with or without Gods help. You may say it was all a coincidence. You may even think I am lying.

But let me review the facts. I had an unsightly wart that kept growing back when removed. It bled profusely all the time. I went through a prayer line. The words spoken were "in the name of Jesus". I fell and the wart was gone. (Couldn't find it on the stake or on the ground). It didn't bleed. The following morning there was no evidence it ever existed, and it never returned. Not hear say! THIS PERSONALLY HAPPENED TO ME.

Youth camp, age 12…. I often was confused by my mom. Here we were living with this abusive crazy lady who seemed absolutely satanic to us kids, and yet she took us to church on occasion, or let us go with others. It was difficult to associate this woman who at church cried and prayed and "and spoke in tongues" with the monster at home who beat us so severely and verbally destroyed us. She never allowed us to go anywhere without her except for church and that was not often. So, you can understand my surprise when a family from church asked her if I could go to a Christian youth camp for a week and she said OK! I wanted desperately to go, but not for the camp, but just to get away from her for a whole week. That sounded like heaven to me!

Camp was OK. Got to sleep late, and breakfast was wonderful. There were lots of fun activities, but I didn't get too involved. I watched a lot. And there was church. Every night. Old fashioned Holy Ghost hellfire and brimstone preaching, and calls to come forward to accept Jesus. I watched many kids my age accept Christ as their savior, and it really did seem to make a difference in the way they acted, but I couldn't bring myself to do the same. I kept wondering who this God was. They said He loved me so much. The one Who said, "suffer the children to come unto me". The One they said would protect me and never forsake me. I wanted to know where in the hell He was when I was being beaten half to death or molested by gay babysitters. It didn't seem to me that He had my best interests at heart. But then, I wasn't there to get to know God. I was simply grateful to be away from the living hell at home for a few days. And the days passed far too quickly. Before I knew it the week had passed, and it was time to go. I was overwhelmed by fear at the thought of going home. Back into the devil's lair.

    We had one last church service that last night. I stood outside the tent looking in, wishing there was something in there that could save me from having to go. But I knew I needed to go because I was worried all week about how my younger siblings were doing without me there to protect them from her. As the service was ending I turned and walked to the river bank and looked up.(the camp was located near a river) I simply said to God, "if you really exist, if You are really there, if you are really powerful enough to speak the world into existence, then surely you can show one little 12 year boy that you are, and you care about me". It was very dark, no moon or stars to light up the area, just the lights from the tent service. The folks that brought me called me and said to come on, it's getting late, and we needed to find the car and head home.

    Once again, its strange what happened. As I turned to head toward the parking area, I noticed my feet felt strange. It was as if I was walking on air. I couldn't feel the ground, yet I could walk OK. As we approached the field where the cars were parked, I looked and the whole sky was lit up. I could clearly see all the cars, and I saw exactly where our car was. Please remember that we are way out in the country, it was pitch black, no moon or stars, and yet I could see clearly. The man and his wife were amazed that I could see exactly where the car was. We went directly to the car; an Oldsmobile I believe it was. The couple's kids got into the back, and I was put in front between them. Then the next strange thing occurred. The light was in the car, but not outside. I could no longer see anything outside the car, but inside it was bright as day. The man was fumbling with the keys because it was dark, but I showed him where the ignition was, and they remarked again how good my eyesight was. And the light began to slowly dim in the car til it was just around me. No one saw the light but me! Once again I thought about going home. But as the light slowly went away, I had the strangest sensation. It felt like a pair of hands were holding me and a peace I had never experienced before soaked into my mind and soul and a great calm came over me. I fell asleep.

Jimmie wake up, you're home, your mom is at the door waiting for you. I was jarred out of a most wonderful sleep and jerked back into reality. But strangely enough, I didn't experience the anxiety I normally had when having to face my mother. I got out of the car and started up the front steps. Mom was standing in the doorway looking annoyed. She spoke to me sharply and told me to get on in the house and get to bed. And then it happened again. When I got close enough for her to see my face she stepped back from the doorway, stared at me, and looked scared for a moment, and very softly said "go to bed Jimmie, its late". I went immediately to bed. She did not come in to check on me. The next day everything was back to the same old insanity that I was used to. Many years later I asked mom if she remembered that night, and why she looked at me strangely. She said yes, I have never forgotten it. Your face was glowing in the dark. Evidently the light was still on me. I was too young to understand what had happened, but I know now God had his hand on me. But God was soon forgotten as the insane abusive way of life continued to take its toll. Now you might say I was a highly imaginative young man, stressed from being afraid. The light was probably residual from the tent. My eyes had adapted well from the darkness. No! I was there! This was not a dream! I did not imagine any of this. THIS ACTUALLY HAPPENED TO ME. Thank you Lord for responding to me.

I should have died but I didn't. When I got my letter telling me I was being drafted, I was working offshore. If you recall this was where my drinking began. I was a flunky crew member on a Lay barge. This is a huge barge with a spool of pipe on one end, and a kitchen, tool room, and sleeping spaces on the other end. There was also a huge dragline welded to the deck on the back corner. This was around 1965. I was 19.

      While we were out, we got word a major hurricane was coming and the tugboat captain who towed the barge out to sea was advised to bring the barge in. Apparently, the barge owner and the tug owner were two different companies. The barge owner told us not to come in yet, so the tugboat left us out there!!! We were just sitting there about a mile from an oil rig bobbing up and down in seas that were slowly getting bigger and bigger. When the barge captain finally decided we should go in, the tugboat said the seas were too rough to get back to us, and we were on our own. The barge had large cables with anchors attached, so we just sat there with the anchors out facing into the waves. Sure enough the hurricane hit us with full force. Huge waves began crashing over the barge like the waves in the perfect storm movie. The water pounded us so hard the kitchen, tool shed, and the sleeping shack was washed overboard. We were all scared and thought we were going to drown. We went up on top of the spool and tied ourselves to eyelets so we would not get washed overboard. The waves got so high they washed completely over the barge, and we were momentarily under water each time. But we kept popping back up after each wave. This went on for several hours up into the night. It was pitch black; we couldn't see anything. Just the howling of the wind and the constant beating of the waves. Suddenly we heard a terrible crashing sound and we all became very afraid. The waves had ripped the dragline loose from the deck leaving a rather large hole which quickly filled with water. This caused the back corner of the barge to sink into the water which caused the right front corner of the barge to lift up higher than the left side. This put a lot of strain on the cable holding the anchor on that side. We were certain we were going to sink.

      Thank goodness the barge was constructed with different sections so that only one corner of the barge filled with water. When we didn't immediately sink, we began to regain some confidence that maybe we might make it out of there. But about that time the cable on the right corner snapped and broke loose from the anchor. This caused the barge to swing around the catty corner to the one anchor and cable still holding us on the left corner. It was the left back corner that was underwater, and this caused the Barge to list to the left. We were almost certain we were going to sink, and we also figured the other cable would eventually break under the stress. We were all crying and begging God for help. We were completely helpless and just hung on for dear life while the waves pounded us all night.

Miraculously, early in the morning the waves began to subside, and the wind began to die down. We were still alive and still afloat. The barge was a complete and total wreck, but it was still hanging in there. Later in the day the tugboat was sent back out to get us. They thought we had sunk but the people on the oil rig some distance away had observed us through the night with binoculars and had called and said we were still afloat. We were told later that they thought we had gone under and sank several times.

We all boarded the tugboat and went to the dock. We got off the boat and got down and kissed the ground. I shall never ever again fear a storm as long as I am on solid ground. We all left and went home and ceased our employment with the barge company as we didn't feel like being employed by people who didn't care enough about us to bring us in. Now I hear you thinking already, that wasn't a miracle, that was a was just an unsettling and unfortunate experience that you had. Possibly. But the cable should have broken, the barge should have sunk. If you had been there, you too would firmly believe God was looking out for me.

Chapter 15

The case of the muted voice....age 20. After my experience at age 12, God was sorta put on a back self for many years. If you recall, I left home at age 14, homeless for a couple years, met my first wife and got married, and finally wound up in the navy. It was during this time in the service that this incident occurred. I was in school at Great Lakes naval training center. On weekends I would go visit family and friends in Rockford Ill, a city seventy miles west of Chicago. One weekend I took my wife and went to see a dear friend. Her name was Ione Hughes. She had helped me when I was fourteen and in the streets. She was a wonderful Godly woman who told me God loved me and would take care of me if I trusted Him. On the Sundays when we were there, we went to church with her. My wife was young and rather outspoken, and freely expressed herself when
annoyed. She had not really wanted to go and was quite vocal about it on the way to church. I kept asking her to keep her voice down, and

not be so hard to get along with. Absolutely the wrong thing to say to her. She went off on me and made it known in no uncertain terms that she would say want she wanted, when she wanted, and how she wanted, and no one could stop her. My wife and I were in the back seat. Mrs. Hughes and her husband were in the front. Mrs. Hughes suddenly turned around in her seat, looked straight at my wife, pointed her finger at her and said, "I rebuke you Satan in the name of Jesus". And something strange happened. My wife kept on speaking, but no sound came out! It took a moment for us to realize what was happening. She kept trying to speak but no sound!! Mrs. Hughes simply smiled and turned around. But my wife was starting to panic a little. I must admit it scared me too. She kept trying to say something till Mrs. Hughes told her to settle down, that she would be able to speak once she was out of the car. We rode in silence to the church. As soon as my wife stepped out of the car her voice immediately returned. She decided it was time to be more agreeable when she saw Mrs. Hughes watching her. She calmed down and was pleasant the rest of the day. She never wanted to discuss what happened and I didn't press the issue. But what had happened?

I believed God closed her mouth. I cannot come up with any other explanation. This is not gossip or some tall tale I heard. I WAS PERSONALLY PRESENT AND OBSERVED THIS AS IT WAS HAPPENING.

If you have a better explanation. Please feel free to contact me and let me know.

God is still looking out for me.... After Boot Camp I went to hospital corps school and from there was sent to the Naval Hospital in Pensacola Florida. While there I applied to go to aviation medicine school and was awaiting my orders when personnel assigned me orders for FMF to go to Vietnam. Another corpsman at the hospital had also applied to a school and was awaiting his orders also. Just before I was scheduled to leave on the FMF orders, my orders for school came in. My name was taken off of the FMF orders and the other Corpsman who was awaiting his orders was put there in my place.

By the time it was time for him to go his orders for school had not come in yet, so he wound up in Vietnam. I was sitting in the hospital cafeteria a few weeks later and one of the Corpsman came in and sat down and looked at me and said you are not going to believe what happened. The corpsman who had been put on my FMF orders and sent in my place had been killed just a few days after arriving in Vietnam. After all this time I still cannot explain how I feel when I think about this. I know, I know, this is just one of those things that happens. Certainly not a miracle? But I firmly believe that this was God looking out for me.

I might interject here that I was like a lot of so-called Christians. You know the type. Claim to be holy but live like heathens. I didn't live like that on purpose, I just never was serious about God and never claimed to be. When I was in my early 20's I was at church watching the folks sing, cry and act really holy, but I knew some of them were using God like a piggy bank and lifeguard. They were all holy when in trouble or need, but when times were good they didn't seem to pay God any attention. I told God I would like to be His friend, but not because I needed Him. I said I would serve Him one day when I had gotten all I needed or wanted on my own. I did not want God to be my backup to take care of all the problems I couldn't handle myself. I don't use people like that, and I certainly didn't want to serve God on that basis. Many years later He reminded me of this long-forgotten decision.

Chapter 16

I mostly lived for myself through my 20's and early 30's. After anesthesia school I was working for a local Mobile, AL. Anesthesia group when several things happened that have deeply affected who I am today. I met a CRNA, Don Wells, who has had more to do with the direction of my life than I would have believed at the time. Don was a Godly man who talked to everyone about Jesus. We became friends and he talked to me often about God. I listened but didn't act too interested. Early one Sunday morning he called me and invited me to church that morning. To my surprise and his, I accepted. We met at First Assembly of God on Michael Blvd in Mobile, AL. And strangely enough, I really enjoyed the service and began to attend on a regular basis. It was here that I saw, heard, and experienced some things that go a long way in supporting why I believe. I will discuss four of them.

The light.... A group of young people had returned from a week at camp and were all fired up about their experience. They were called upon the platform by the podium and encouraged to talk about their week. Guess what I saw that no one else was aware of??? I saw the same light on them that I saw at camp when I was 12 years old!!!!! And how do I know no one else saw it? I asked my wife who was standing next to me where the white light was coming from, and she didn't see it. My good friend Don didn't see it either. But I saw the light that day in more ways than one.

Tongues.... I had grown up around Pentecost and although I was familiar with the practice, I personally didn't believe in it and thought it was fake. I watched my mother speak in tongues and then beat the ever-loving hell out of us. No thanks, I wasn't interested in that crap. But I did enjoy Pentecostal services because they were less boring than other denominations I had attended. The music and song songs were uplifting, and I enjoyed singing. They were familiar songs from my childhood, and it just felt good to join in even though I can't carry a tune in a bucket. It was during a praise and worship service that I was singing and feeling the presence of God that I heard the most beautiful melodious singing in tongues that I have ever heard. I looked around to see who it was with such a lovely voice, and suddenly realized it was me! I was shocked! Something I totally didn't believe in was happening to me. And it was coming out spontaneously with no effort or intent on my part! My wife was looking strangely at me because she heard it too and could hardly believe that beautiful sound was coming out of me considering my complete lack of singing ability. Wow! Do I believe in tongues now? Absolutely. But while I still believe that a lot of it is fake, I do believe it is real. Many years later I had surgery and my wife told me I was speaking in tongues as I was waking up. I don't recall doing it, but I felt absolutely wonderful when I was finally awake. Is speaking in tongues real? Some think it's a lot of hocus-pocus while others absolutely believe it's real. Whether you think it's for real or not doesn't matter. I am simply telling you what happened to me and that is one of many reasons why I believe.

Slain in the spirit…. If you are not familiar with Pentecost this one is going to sound absolutely insane. Pentecostals believe that the spirit of God can come upon you so strong that you can be rendered almost unconscious. When this happens you usually fall to the floor and can be oblivious to your surroundings for a period of time from 1-2 minutes up to 30 minutes or more. This most often occurs when a person is being prayed for. This too is something I never believed in for much the same reasons I didn't believe in tongues. I always believed they fell because they were pushed, and they stayed down because it was "expected."

    We had gone to church one Sunday night to hear a visiting evangelist preach. At a point in the service, he asked if anyone had a need to come forward and he would pray for them. Several went down, self-included. This man did not push me or anyone else. He simply put a dab of oil on his forefinger and lightly touched my forehead and said, "In the name of Jesus". I was suddenly aware of being flat on my back on the floor and felt absolutely wonderful. I opened my eyes and saw my wife standing over me. I could hear a lot of people praying. I slowly got up and walked back to my seat and sat down. My wife looked very concerned and asked if I was hurting anywhere. No, I felt great! She was concerned because she had been raised Episcopalian and had never seen anything like this before. She said I fell straight back and hit my head so hard on the floor that she was afraid I had been knocked out. I was down for about 20 minutes, but it seemed like only seconds to me. I felt incredibly well and had no pain anywhere. I know you think I am really crazy now. I'm ok with that. I'm just telling you what happened and why I believe this is a legitimate experience although I still believe some of it is fake.

    A side note to this experience. I was a good old navy guy with a colorful vocabulary. In spite of attending church, I had not quite quit engaging in varying degrees of profanity. But after this experience I stopped cursing without realizing I had done so. A week later my wife noted that I had not cursed for a whole week and admitted that there just might be something real about this "slain in the spirit stuff". I'm not asking you to believe in this stuff, I'm just telling you what happened to me and is one of many reasons why I believe.

Chapter 17

The $2000.00 pledge....The church I attended needed to expand and asked for pledges to raise the money for the project. The money was needed in 90 days. The pastor said to pray and ask God the amount we should give. He said even if we were not sure about where the money would come from, that God would provide it. The Bible says to test God in our giving and the blessing bestowed on us would be so great we cannot contain it and it will spill out on those around us. I am not sure I believed that at the time, but decided I would give it a try. I prayed about it and the sum of two thousand dollars came to mind. I was uncomfortable with this at first because in the early 1980's this was a significant amount of money. But I made the pledge because I had an above average income and was confident I could come up with the money even if God didn't lend a helping hand. To be perfectly honest it made me feel like a big shot to give so much. And I thought it would be a good way to test Gods Word.

Time passed and I had forgotten about the pledge. We had incurred some unexpected expenses and my cash flow was running a bit low. You can imagine my initial panic when the pastor reminded us of the pledges were due the following Sunday. I did not have the money. I decided I get a loan and pay it back over time. Simple solution! Maybe?

We worked on commission at work and were paid once a month on the 1st which just so happened to fall on that week the pledge was due. When I saw my check, I was absolutely amazed. My check was two thousand dollars more than last month's check! Hey, you might say, you work on commission and had a good month at work. Doesn't sound like a miracle to me. How about a little more info. Not only was my check up two thousand dollars, all the other CRNA's checks were up two thousand dollars from the previous month. Over 20 people all had a good month? Not so. We felt like a mistake had been made and contacted the office to see what was going on. We were told the checks were correct. But we were told by the office manager that it was unusual. So much so that when the computer printed out the checks, she thought there was a big mistake and ran them through the computer again with the same results. They decided the computer had a glitch and redid all the figures by hand. Guess what! Same result. And so we were paid! God had intervened.

I was eager to find out if God played a role in this or if in fact, we all had just "Had a good month". Most of us kept records of our cases because of the way we were paid. Proving a good month should be easy. I averaged 90-95 cases per month as did most of the other CRNA's. I checked the previous month's record and compared it to this month's record. They were approximately the same. Only a couple of cases difference. Absolutely not enough to generate two thousand dollars, a couple of hundred at the most. The following month I compared my records again with the previous two months and they were the same. Approximately the same number and types of cases. This incident occurred once! When the pledge was due!

It had never happened before, and it never happened again in the eight years I worked there! God had honored my pledge and provided just as the Bible said He would. And it spilled out on everyone around me. Just as the Bible said it would. If you have a better explanation, please feel free to contact me and explain. This personally happened to me and is one of many reasons why I believe.

There were some other things that happened during my mid 30's church going stage that are significant. I will discuss four. The first two involve just me, and the other two involve patients of mine. Obviously, I can't give names and dates for the patients, but I can certainly tell you what I personally observed.

The case of the spinning truck.... I had gone to Pensacola, Florida and was returning home in my Toyota pickup truck. It was pouring rain and I could barely see the road. I was on I-10 heading west just past the Florida state line. I had slowed down to about 60 miles an hour, but it was still much too fast for the weather conditions. There were two 18-wheeler trucks and several cars around me. I was in the left lane and the trucks were in the right lane approximately a hundred feet apart. There was a car in front of me and several behind. We were slowly passing the big trucks. And then it happened. I hydroplaned. My front tires lost all contact with the pavement. My truck began a slow turn to the right, and I spun in a complete circle while at the same time sliding toward the right lane where the big trucks were. Keep in mind the rain is so heavy I can barely see the other vehicles. My truck started another complete turn as it slid through the space between the two big trucks. I was headed toward the side of the hi-way with my truck halfway into a second complete turn when I realized there was a very steep embankment I was heading toward. I knew as soon as my tires slid off the blacktop and hit the mud the truck would flip over and roll down the embankment. Also keep in mind the truck is moving forward at approximately 55-60 mph while it's spinning. When this whole episode began, I knew I was in trouble, and asked God to please help me. By now the truck had completed its second turn and had reached the side of the road. I was seconds from rolling down the embankment when I cried out "I need You now! And slammed my fist down on the dash. And then it happened! The truck suddenly stopped like a giant hand had grabbed it. I was sitting on the side of the road out of the way of traffic facing west just inches from the end of the pavement on the right side of my vehicle. To passing traffic I probably looked like I had just pulled off to the side of the road because of the rain. I was safe and my truck was headed in the right direction. Let's make sure we understand just what happened. Two complete turns moving forward at 50-60 in blinding rain and the truck stopped instantly? After I calmed down, I pulled back on the interstate at a much slower speed and went home. A bit shaken, but most grateful to God for intervening. This happened to me and is one of the many reasons why I believe.

Chapter 18

    The heart attack...or was it? During the time I was attending church and trying not to be a heathen, I had quit drinking even though my wife continued to do so. One evening our neighbor threw a little party and we attended. There was lots of booze and lots of spicy Mexican food. I had not intended to drink, but my wife and others kept pushing me to "have just one drink to be sociable". And I did. The problem was I didn't stop with one. I didn't get sloppy drunk like I used to do, but I certainly had more than I should have. And I ate way too much hot spicy food. Not a good combination.

    We went home feeling way better than I should have. I was getting ready for bed when I suddenly had a crushing pain in my chest, and I couldn't breathe! Everything started going black and I fell to the floor beside the bed. As I lay there, I felt like I was in a big black void and rapidly falling down, down down! I was terrified because I thought I was having a heart attack and was dying. I couldn't speak, but in my mind I started crying out the Name of Jesus. Suddenly I stopped falling and was just suspended in this black void. But as I continued to say Jesus, Jesus, Jesus I began to rise. Slowly I began see light in the distance and each time I said Jesus, I got closer to the light. Suddenly I was awake lying on the floor with the chest pain slowly subsiding and breathing becoming easier. I wasn't dead!! I was very weak but managed to get up and lie down on the bed. I was jerked awake by the alarm clock telling me it was time for me to get up and go to work. I had obviously fallen asleep. I felt OK when I sat up, so I got dressed and went to work. As soon as I got there, I talked to a couple of the doctors about my experience the night before. They didn't seem too concerned and said I was most likely having an esophageal spasm from the alcohol and spicy food. They said it was common and felt just like a heart attack. I felt fine and they said not to worry about it. So I didn't. At least not then.

A couple of hours later I had a patient asleep on the or table. I was standing there watching the monitor and thinking about the previous night and started thinking how stupid I was to think I was having a heart attack. After all I was in my mid 30's, in great physical condition and never had chest pain before. How foolish of me to be crying and begging God for help when there was nothing wrong with me! And then it happened.

I suddenly had severe chest pain and I couldn't breathe. I realized immediately my mistake and cried to God to forgive me for the previous night and for dismissing Him. The pain stopped instantly, and I could breathe normally. I never again had chest pain and shortness of breath like I experienced that previous night and following morning. Sounds crazy I know, but this happened to me and is one of many reasons why I believe.

The case of the disappearing tumor.... Part of our job as CRNA's involves going to see the patient the night before surgery. I went to see a patient scheduled for the next morning to introduce myself and obtain some necessary history to plan for the anesthetic. It provides an opportunity to establish a rapport with the patient and answer their questions about anesthesia.

As I entered the room, I observed an older slender lady sitting up in the bed. She broke out with an awesome smile and greeted me like an old friend. I introduced myself and told her I would be providing anesthesia for her tumor removal. She said she was so glad to meet me and was looking forward to the surgery, but there would be no tumor to remove by morning. I asked her what made her think it would be gone? She said God was going to remove it.

    I asked her why she was having the surgery if she knew the tumor would be gone. She said it was necessary as a witness to family, friends, and her doctors. Of course, I admit I was skeptical because she was a small lady, and the tumor was large enough to see and feel. She showed me the bump in her abdomen and assured me again that it would be gone by morning. I finished my visit and left.

    They brought her to the OR in the morning. She had been sedated but was still awake and very pleasant. We put her on the or table, hooked up the monitors and put her to sleep. I was sitting behind an ether screen and was not observing the surgery. Shortly after opening the abdomen, the surgeon stepped back from the table, and asked us to double check the patient's identification. We confirmed that the right patient was on the table. He went over and looked at the patients Xray, then returned to table and reexamined the patient's abdomen. He then asked the circulating nurse to check in the doctors' lounge and see if there was a surgeon available to come and give him an opinion about the patient.

A surgeon came in and asked what he could do to help. The patient's doctor asked him to scrub in and examine the patient's abdomen, which he did. After a couple of minutes, he said there wasn't anything abnormal that he could find and asked why he was called in. The patient's surgeon told him to examine the X-ray and tell him his opinion about what he saw. After a minute he asked whose X-ray it was. We told him it belonged to the patient on the table. He asked how old the X-ray was. When he was told it was less than a week old, he laughed and said "I don't know who is on the table, but this is not her X-ray. The X-ray shows a rather large tumor, but the patient on the table does not have a tumor anywhere in her abdomen ". He turned and left the OR. The room was completely silent. Her surgeon examined her abdomen one more time and sewed her up. It was obvious the surgeon was deeply affected by what had just happened. We woke her up and took her to the recovery room.

The next day I went to see the patient to make sure there were no post-op anesthesia problems, which is standard practice for all surgeries. When I walked into her room, she gave me that big smile and said, "I told you so". She was wide awake and said she felt great and had absolutely no pain. I didn't know what to say and she knew I was deeply affected by this experience. She told me this was what God had told her to do and it served as a witness to those who needed to see it. I saw it. I needed to see it. Remembering it strengthens my faith and it is one of many reasons why I believe.

      Twelve hours to make things right… I was at work and was given a case that just been brought into the emergency room and rushed to surgery. The patient was a woman in her mid-forties who had suffered a ruptured abdominal aortic aneurysm. Her skin was dusky gray, her pupils were fixed and dilated, and she initially had no blood pressure. She looked dead. But her heart was still beating so we proceeded with surgery.

      I managed to get her blood pressure up and her color improved, but her eyes remained fixed and dilated. I feared she had gone too long with no pressure and had brain damage and was not going to survive. While the surgeons worked to fix the problem, I began to wonder who she was and what her status was in life. This was during the time I was going to church and trying to live right.

I wondered if she was a Christian, if she was spiritually ready to die. I suddenly got a strong urge to pray for her. I put my hands on her forehead and asked God to intervene on her behalf. I asked if she was indeed to die, would He allow her brain to wake up enough to pray and make things right with Him before He took her. Her eyes remained fixed and dilated, but her color and vital signs returned to normal. But she didn't wake up at the end of the surgery, so we took her to the recovery room with the endotracheal tube still in place and put her on a ventilator. We did not expect her to live. And then it happened.

About thirty minutes after arriving in the recovery room this patient who appeared to be in a coma suddenly opened her eyes, sat up in bed, pulled out her endotracheal tube, and began to talk to the nurses! When I heard what happened I went immediately to see her. She was awake, talking and seemed quite normal. I asked her how she felt. She said her stomach hurt but otherwise she felt fine. I was amazed. I had a patient waiting for me, so I had to go but resolved to come back later or tomorrow as time permitted and talk to her about her spiritual condition.

    I came in early the next morning so I would have an opportunity to talk to her. Her bed site was empty, so I assumed they had sent the patient to a room. When I inquired as to where she had been sent, I was shocked at the answer. The nurse said the lady did fine all day. She was alert and talking and seemed to be making a remarkable recovery. Approximately twelve hours after arriving in the recovery room she was sitting up talking when suddenly she stopped speaking, her eyes rolled back, and she fell back flat on the bed. She was dead!!! Of course, they called a code and tried to resuscitate her, but she was gone. I desperately wished I had talked with her the night before, but I took comfort in the fact I prayed for her, and God gave her twelve hours to make things right. It doesn't matter if you believe this or not. I do, and it is one of many reasons why I believe.

    These things happened during the couple of years I faithfully attended church. Life was good, and my wife and I were happy. The kids were doing great, and I could only see blue skies in the future. But I did and said something so dumb that even now I can hardly believe I said something so incredibly stupid.

Chapter 19

This was during the time I was involved in financial services and had just quit my anesthesia job to do this full time. When I quit, I cashed out my retirement funds with the anesthesia group and used the money to help with living expenses while I was building up my income from rental properties and getting clients for IRA's, insurance, etc. Being a "good Christian", I decided I needed to give some of this money to a new church I was attending.

I met with the pastor and the minister of music and presented them with a check for $6000.00. Of course, there was a lot "thank you Jesus" going on because this was a lot of money in the 80's. We talked a bit about how the church was growing, and about how lucky we were to live in a country where we had free access to the Bible. And then it happened.

Stupid me said I had read so much of the Bible and was so close to God that I could survive as a Christian if I never read another bible, and I could withstand whatever satan could throw my way. Wow, it's like I was trying to raise stupid to an art form. I just know Satan ran immediately to God and said, "did you just hear what that stupid little arrogant human said"? Please, please, please give me a shot at this one!

And guess what? I think he did. Looking back, I can see my demise began at that point. My life began to slowly fall apart. My business ventures began to fail. My marriage began to fail. And I started drinking and drugging again. And the downward spiral began. Over the next few years, I lost my properties, my wife, my children, my job, my precious money, all gone. But silly me thought I was doing great. Addiction does that to a person.

It "robs you of all that's good, till there's nothing left to save, till you're all alone, your life is gone, and you have become its total slave." On the surface I appeared to be doing ok, but underneath where no one could see, my soul was dying. Of course, this decline didn't happen immediately, but slowly over several years. And God in His forgiving nature gave me a great opportunity to make things right again. But I neglected to take it. He spoke to me.

In the mid 80's. I bought a nice home in west Mobile, Alabama. Three acres, 2800 sf home with fireplace, 20x40 pool, big carport and only a short distance from Walmart. What more could a fella possibly want? The neighbors were party hardy types, and it didn't take long for us to become good drinking buddies. (Same neighbor when I had my "heart attack").

But I was doing well. I was educated, had a great job, had nice cars, and had money. Had all I thought I had ever wanted. After all, when I was young only rich folks had what I had. I was home one afternoon and decided to lay out in the pool. I was lying on a small raft with my eyes closed. It was a beautiful day; the sun was shining, and all was right with my world. I was thinking about where I had come from and all that I now had and was feeling quite proud of myself for getting it all on my own. And then it happened.

A voice spoke to me and said, "how about now". I immediately looked up and to the right to where the voice came from. There was no one there. But I was looking into the eastern sky, and I had distinctly heard a voice that seemed to come from that direction. Or did I.? Was it a real voice or an impression in my mind? No, I heard it. And immediately my mind flashed back to many years ago when I had promised God I would serve Him when I didn't need Him. When I got it all on my own, then I would serve him. I got out of the pool and walked around pondering what had just happened. I was a bit shaken and decided I needed a drink to calm my nerves. And drink I did because I didn't want to deal with God at the moment. Besides, I didn't really need Him. I basically blew Him off and continued down the path the deceiver had placed before me.

Looking back now I can see how quickly I fell into the abyss of the deceived. It had only been a few months since my challenge to the devil, and it looked like he was winning. But as I look back, I remember the voice saying, "how about now" and I know it was God speaking to me. It's OK if you think I'm crazy. If you do it doesn't matter. This happened to me and is one of the reasons why I believe.

The beginning of the end…. I continued this dance through life alone. My wife had left and taken the kids, but as I had written earlier, I was good. Wine, women and song kept me going. Everybody thought I was great. I worked hard and kept up a good appearance for all concerned. But too much stress and emotional strain combined with an ever-deepening sense of loneliness began to seriously erode my will to live. I knew I couldn't keep going like I was but didn't know how to stop. I was an alcoholic/drug addict.

I refused to admit this to myself, but I knew if something didn't give, I would die, and my children would suffer. I decided to lighten my load and sold all my rental properties thinking this would help. And it did. But the IRS came down on me like a load of bricks. As I recall it was around 35 thousand plus interest they wanted. I didn't have it. This was a lot of money 30 years ago (still is) and I was at a loss as to how to deal with it. I was skating on thin ice no matter which direction I turned. But God stepped in as He always does and nudged me in the right direction. One night I was drinking and drugging a bit more than usual.

I was driving south on Shillinger Road in Mobile. And then it happened. I suddenly saw what I thought was a giant fireball heading toward me. I panicked and turned around and drove as fast as my truck would go and came to a stop at the intersection of Airport and Shillinger, a major intersection surrounded by shopping centers. I pulled over in the parking area and sat for a while. It was midnight, and as I was sitting there the radio announcer said they were signing off as soon as the national

anthem played. I decided to sit there and listen to it. And then it happened again.
It didn't play. A voice came out of the radio and said "if you can hear this He has come and gone. You were left behind." I was frozen with fear. I looked around and saw I was the only vehicle in an area that always has traffic 24/7. I truly thought the Lord had returned and I was left because I was lost in the abyss.

      Suddenly I remembered my cousin who was a preacher. If she was gone then I would know it was true. It was midnight but I called her anyway. You have no idea how relieved I was to hear her voice. I told her what happened. She prayed for me and told me to get some sleep. In a moment of clarity I realized I needed help. I called the board of nursing, told them I had a problem and agreed to enter treatment. This was in the fall of 1996.

Chapter 20

My recovery vs the IRS: I went to a treatment center just outside of Birmingham Alabama for evaluation of my addiction. After a few days of tests and interviews they told me I was much too sick to benefit from their program and recommended I go to Talbot recovery center in Atlanta GA. Considering my life and my condition they felt I would benefit more from a 90 day program geared toward medical professionals. I agreed and entered that program in October 1996. Over the course of the next 18 weeks I died to myself. The man that left is who I have grown to be.

The first few weeks were difficult. I had only agreed to go to keep my license and be able to work after I got out. I was having a hard time accepting that I was who they said I was. Arrogant? Selfish? Self-centered? Manipulating? A liar? A cheat? Insensitive and uncaring? Always wanting things to be done my way? Blaming others for all my problems? Pretending to be better than I was? Basically, a big fake! And blamed all of it on my poor mother for not treating me right!

Boohoo, poor little me, and I was dealing with the guilt and shame of my miserable existence by drinking and drugging myself into an early grave! Just who in the hell did they think they were talking to! I was smarter than most, was highly educated and made a lot of money! How could I possibly be such a failure? But here I was in a drunken junkie camp with lots of very intelligent folks with tons of education and the ability to earn incredible sums of money! And our lives were all in the toilet!

As I wrote earlier in my drinking/drugging history a little light came on one day when I was talking to myself as I passed my counselor. He stopped me and said I would never get well until I let go and Let God take over. And I realize now God had already begun to work on my behalf long before I arrived at the treatment center.

When I went to Atlanta for treatment this IRS mess was still hanging over my head. I was scared to deal with them and scared not too. They were threatening to take what little I had left and make me pay them for the rest of my life! They were charging me 12% interest and the balance owed was just going up and up. But I knew I had to let them know where I was and what was happening and why I would not be available for a while. The second day there I called the IRS hotline to try and find out who I needed to talk to. And then it happened. Each time someone answered they would transfer me to another number. This happened 8 times.

I got transferred all over the USA until on the eight call a man listened to my tale of woe and then said some things that could only be the hand of God at work. He told me he was very familiar with Talbot recovery center. His mom had been through the program and came out a new woman. He completely understood my situation and told me not to worry, he was going to fix it for me. He put my case on hold, stopped the interest and gave me his phone number. He said to call him after I completed my program, and he would assist me with setting up a payment schedule that I could afford. I did, and he did. Just one more reason to believe God was looking out for me.

After my encounter with my counselor in the hall I began to seriously look at myself and all the character flaws that made up my mangled personality. I started a dialogue with God that continues to this very day. And I began to change. I fessed up and admitted that most of my difficult life experiences were indeed my fault. I began to understand that my difficult childhood didn't have to define who I was. And I did something that was the key to getting free. Something I never thought I would ever do. I forgave my mom.

    I was released in February 1997 and went home as a brand-new person. I still had some growing to do but I was finally free from "a mind full of anger, a heart turned to stone, unable to love and always alone". Truly God was fixing me! This all happened to me and is one of many reasons I believe.

Chapter 21

I wish I could tell you life was wonderful from this point on. I wish I could say I never did anything stupid again. I wish I could say I recognized the voice of God in my life. But obviously Satan and God were still in discussion about me. Yes, Satan had taken me down a few notches. But it was only because God allowed it. I guess my spiritual repair job needed to be tested. If you recall from my previous addiction history, I did well for five years. I went to AA/NA meetings, went to church, studied my Bible and healed mentally, and emotionally, and grew spiritually. Or at least I thought I had. Enter a third wife. I have already described that fiasco in the wives section. But how could I have possibly gotten myself into that situation if I was doing so well? Enter the light.

The Bible says Satan comes to us as an angel of light, beautiful in every way. We are so taken in that we really believe it is God Himself making a way for us. And down the path we go. Headlong to the slaughter. Had I really been a mature Christian I would have recognized that the relationship was not entered into in a manner pleasing to God. The progression of the relationship did not line up scripturally.

I would have seen that the life she was living did not line up with what she was saying about her belief in God. I was blinded by my own wishes and desires to the point I did not see God's wishes and desires for my life going forward. Unfortunately, this is what happens to so many of us. Sometimes I think God allowed this so I could learn the difference between His voice and satans. If a situation does not line up with the Word of God, it is not God speaking. It's that simple. It was a hard lesson, but I learned.

After four years of absolute hell, I finally surrendered, and removed myself from that insanity. Thankfully I did not start drinking again and continued throughout that situation to reach out to God daily for help. I could not have survived otherwise. That experience reinforced my belief that God is looking out for me even when I am stupid.

I was now by myself, but not alone. God's presence surrounded me and lifted me up in a way that's hard to explain. I expressed to Him my wants and desires for my future, but agreed to leave it all in His Hands and accept

His will for my life going forward. I also believe that Satan realized he was not going to win and slipped away to try another day what he had not accomplished. My destruction! And he did try again. Later. Try being the key word. I went to church, read my Bible, went to work, spent time with my son and was content with life. I vowed to never marry again unless God personally sent her to me. And I set down the conditions that would have to be met for that to happen. They were specific enough that I felt safe that I would never have to endure another woman as long as I lived! Happy and free at last! Content with life at last! The Bible says that who the Son has set free is free indeed. And free I was!! And then it happened!

God's plan for man is that he is not alone. Although I was willing to accept God's will for my life, I didn't really think He was serious about me not being alone. I had been alone my entire life. No matter how many were around me, I was always alone. I tried to fill the void with drugs and alcohol. Didn't work. I tried with women. Didn't work. I tried with work, projects, schemes of all kinds. Didn't work. Only God can fill the void. And once He fills the empty hole in your soul that only He can fill you suddenly find that you are open to relationships that are proper and fulfilling. And

I prayed for what I needed. I just didn't know what I needed, but God did. He sent Johanna.

Chapter 22

If you recall, Johanna is discussed in the wives section. But a review here is warranted. For me to accept a future spouse she needed to be a faithful Christian who believed in tithing, 5'7", blue eyes, dark hair, long legs, short waist, weigh less than 125 lbs., frugal, soft spoken, slow to anger, trustworthy, and love God more than me. She would have to walk up to me and say God sent me. And, of course, all men know this woman doesn't exist. I was perfectly safe.

I guess I had forgotten that God is in control of our lives, and He works best when we turn our will over to Him which is what I had finally done. I was standing in the back of the church during a praise and worship service when a woman I had often observed 'singing' in sign language walked up to me. She said God spoke to her and sent her a message for me. She handed me a slip of paper that she had written on what she felt the Lord wanted me to know. Written there was what I needed and had prayed for.

The message essentially was God loved me and was going to provide the family and love I had always wanted and needed. I had grown spiritually and been healed of the pain of my childhood. It was time.

Long story short, Johanna and I were married 7 months later. I wish I could say it was the most blissful journey to start. God may have put us together, but he was still working with flawed human beings. We each had children and baggage that needed to be blended into what God had planned. The rough edges had to be sanded off. Over the next few years, the blending and sanding was in full force! A strange blend of pain and bliss. I am not sure we would have survived had we not followed God's way of dealing with conflict. But we did. We were committed to our relationship. We were committed to God. Prayer and commitment are an awesome answer to conflict. It got us through the sanding phase and made the blending much easier and rewarding. Today we are secure and strong in our commitment to God and to each other. Johanna is a wonderful woman, and I would not want to live without her. After a lifetime of insanity I have fully surrendered to the amazingly good life that God has provided me. And this is one of the many reasons I believe.

Perhaps another recap is worth taking a look at. I was raised in an insane and abusive environment. I ran away and was essentially homeless for several years. Got married. Got drafted, did my stint with the military. Did odd jobs after service and finally ended up going to college. Got divorced. Married again. Became somewhat prosperous , but also an alcoholic and drug addict. Got divorced again. Drank my prosperity away, and wound up in a drunken junkie camp. Got reborn!!. I was getting well, but was still stupid. Got married again, lived in hell for a while. Finally wised and let God take control of my life. Still have to deal with a storm now and then, but it's mostly smooth sailing these days. The road from hell to heaven can be long and rocky, but it's worth the trip. Today is good. Johanna and I live in a nice home on 20 acres that is paid for. We are financially secure. We have family and friends that we can enjoy and depend on. I love and adore Johanna. She is a bit peculiar, but she is my gift from God and I will always honor her as such. I have come a long way since being lost and alone and sleeping in an old abandoned car. And by now you should have a good idea why I believe.

Chapter 23

My journey to belief was not all determined by personal experiences. I have read several books about the resurrection of Jesus written by former atheists who became believers after investigating the facts surrounding His life. The evidence is almost overwhelming to anyone who sees it with an unbiased mind. I am not going to overwhelm you with a mountain of evidence, but bring to your attention some interesting facts and tidbits I have discovered in my search for proof that Jesus was who He said He was.

Of the several books I have read I found two that I found very persuasive. One was "The case for Christ "by Lee Strobel. He was an atheist who researched Jesus to prove to his wife it was all fake. He eventually was converted by the evidence. His books can be found in many places where books are sold. The other is "The Archko Volume", "the archeological writings of the Sanhedrin & Talmuds of the Jews". This is an awesome and eye-opening book that details much information taken directly from actual official documents written at the time of Christ's crucifixion.

These documents are maintained in Vatican archives, and the official historical records maintained by the Jews in Jerusalem. I strongly urge anyone serious about learning about Jesus to get and read this book.

I have heard the stories about the birth of Christ, the normal Christmas stories, the Shepherds, the angels singing, etc., etc.... But I didn't know that the Jewish priests sent a rabbi named Gamaliel to Bethlehem to interview the residents about the night Jesus was born. They had heard about the birth and had investigated. They interviewed the Shepherds that saw the star and heard the angels sing. What I didn't know was that more people than the shepherds saw and heard the angels! All the people in Bethlehem saw and heard them. The local rabbi saw and heard them. The local contingent of Roman soldiers saw them! A documented report was sent to the Sanhedrin detailing these findings. This report is in the archives in Jerusalem. I didn't know Pontus Pilate knew Jesus prior to the trial and had been protecting Him. This is why he knew Jesus was innocent.

I didn't know Jesus appeared to the chief priest Caiaphas after the resurrection. Caiaphas was locked in his chambers with a guard outside because he had been informed that Jesus was alive, and he feared Jesus would kill him. Jesus appeared to him and told him not to be afraid. Then He simply disappeared. This incident is detailed in Caiaphas's letter of resignation to the Sanhedrin. He resigned as chief priest because he finally knew Jesus was who He said He was. This letter of resignation is in the archives in Jerusalem.

This book is so full of documented information that points to Jesus being who He said He was that I was overwhelmed reading it. It's hard to deny the information presented because it all comes from hard documentation. I have always tended to believe people with an unbiased opinion.

One of the stories in the book was about a retired Roman general who was also an historian. In his career conquering other countries for Rome, he would keep a diary of information about the countries and their culture. Concerning Israel, he noted that he was not too impressed with the county, but there was a man there that was worth mentioning. He said this man had a unique ability to control the weather. Chew on that for a while. I urge you to find and read these two books. There are many others, but these had the greatest effect on me. And they are one of many reasons I believe.

There are other bits of information and occurrences that have helped form my opinion about God and my belief in Him. I will present a few of them now but it is in no way a complete list of the many things I have seen or experienced that help my belief.

The blood ......an archeologist, Ron Wyatt, January 6th, 1982, at 2pm found some blood in a cavern underneath the place where Jesus was crucified. He also found what he believed was the ark of the covenant. He believed the blood of Jesus had drained down through the cracks in the rocks and fell on the ark. He took a sample of the dried blood to a lab in Jerusalem to be analyzed. The report is truly amazing. It was human blood. The blood cells were still alive in spite of being very old and dried out. And the chromosome count was very interesting. Humans normally have 46 chromosomes. 23 from the mother, and 23 from the father. This blood only had 24. 23 were maternal, meaning they were from the mother, but only 1 was paternal, meaning from the father. Feel free to go online to Ron's website and read this amazing story of discovery.

The disciples …. twelve men personally lived and experienced Jesus. Several wrote what they actually saw and knew to be true. They died horrible deaths rather than deny that Jesus was who he said He was. All they had to do to live was to say it was all a lie they made up and agree that Jesus was not who He said He was. That's it! No horrible death! They get to live! You might get 2-3 people crazy enough to die unnecessarily, but not 12. Considering the manner of their deaths, all different, all painful, all horrible, you will not find 12. At least 1 or 2, but most likely more would wimp out and give up the 'TRUTH' because only a fool would knowingly die for a lie. And there were many more who went to their death rather than deny Jesus was who He said He was. The apostle Paul was killing Christians when Jesus appeared to him, and he instantly changed and became one of the greatest witnesses for Jesus that has ever lived. He too suffered much and died rather than deny that Jesus was indeed the Christ, the One who came to set us free from the bondage of sin and give eternal life to all who believed.

The Big Bang…. I went to college. They told us about evolution. They told us about the Big Bang. I was not a believer at that point and listened with an open mind. A lot of what they said made sense. But some of it did not. They told me the entire universe, all the planets, stars and everything we can see came from a small ball of matter the size of a basketball. It exploded and everything came to an end in seconds. Now I smoked a lot of weed in college, but not even LSD, and mushroom tea can mess you up enough to believe that piece of manure. It's easier to believe an intelligent being created everything.

In fact, the order in the universe points to that very fact. Many years later I was able to read about and study DNA and became even more convinced of a designer/creator. But don't take my word for it. Get a copy of the book 'the Evolution Cruncher' by Vance Ferrell. Read it, ponder on the evidence, and if you still want to believe in the big bang and evolution, go for it. But don't ask me to. The Bible says that God's people perish from lack of knowledge. But knowledge doesn't just fall into your lap, you have to go find it. And I have, and that's why I believe.

The Bible.... This book contains many prophecies written hundreds of years prior to Jesus's birth that are so numerous that it's impossible for one person to fulfill all of them and yet He did.

When I was around 72 yrs. old, I developed a painful condition in my left foot called plantar fasciitis. It was incredibly painful to the point of being difficult to walk. I purchased a special shoe, but still endured severe pain especially in the mornings. I limped around like a wounded animal. This went on for several weeks and seemed to actually be getting worse. It was probably time to seek medical help. I was limping into work one morning and suddenly stopped and looked at my foot. I decided to try something that I wish I thought of much sooner. I commanded the pain to stop in the name of Jesus. And then it happened. The pain stopped instantly. Gone. Never returned. I wish I could explain how one feels when they trust God and good things happen. Just know it helps me to believe.

As previously noted, I am an anesthetist. I put people to sleep for surgical procedures. Part of our job is to maintain the patients' vital signs within a normal range. (Blood pressure and pulse). Most of the time this is easy to do.

But sometimes due to health issues this can be a little more difficult. I have had on several occasions to give drugs and fluids more than usually to keep the patient's vital signs within an acceptable level. Sometimes we can barely keep them where we want them. I have had several occasions where I was having difficulty keeping the blood pressure up and I simply said, 'Lord I could use a little help with this one'. And then it would happen. The heart rate and blood pressure would stabilize, and I had no further issues. It brings new meaning to the phrase 'flying in on a wing and a prayer'. It could be a coincidence, but this has happened more than once. I think it happens because I believe.

Something that I experience every time I go to work also helps me immensely. There is a large parking lot behind the hospital where I park. I get out of my vehicle and looking toward the hospital I see the buildings, the many vehicles, the pavement and other structures. I am immediately reminded that all these things were designed and created by some creative thinking person or persons who saw a need and created those things that would fulfill the need. Intelligent design and creation. I know it happened because I can see the end result. I also see people, trees, grass, and a variety of shrubs growing everywhere. Why does the world around me believe that all the 'stuff' was designed and created but not the people, trees, and shrubs? Is humanity that stupid? There was a first car, a first building, a first tree, person and shrub. Why do we believe in everything that we created, but not that everything we have no ability to create has a creator??? Truly we have raised stupid to an art form!

Chapter 24

In the beginning I said what one believes about God depends a lot on our source of information about Him, and whether or not we find our source to be credible. I have previously mentioned a couple of books that I read that helped me immensely which you might consider getting you started, but most of what we believe comes from those who we have witnessed in our life and what we think about them. In addition to my extensive reading and personal experiences, I have known many people who I respect and value their life and opinions. They too experienced a journey to God that I deeply respect. I will mention a few and the effect they had on me. You probably know someone you respect and will understand why I feel the way I do about them.

My aunt Jackie.... During the intense abuse of my childhood Jackie was the only one who ever stood up for me. She was my mom's younger sister. She would visit occasionally and would stay a few days each time. She was aware of her sister's temper, and her insane abuse of her children. For the most part she stayed out of the way but would intervene when she feared mom would severely injure us. She could usually get her calmed down and away from us. But she paid for her interference. One day while Jackie was ironing clothes, mom had me down beating with her fist. Jackie grabbed her arm and screamed at her to stop before she killed me.

Mom turned me loose, grabbed the hot iron and pressed it into Jackie's face. Jackie left the next day and I do not recall seeing her again before I left home. During the times she was with us she would hold me and tell me God loved me and I had value and worth. Many years later I would visit her often and she was always talking about Jesus and how I needed to trust Him with my life. When she talked about God her face would light up and she seemed so happy. What was so confusing to me was she was dirt poor and lived in a project in New Orleans, and yet she was one of the happiest people I have ever known. I was heartbroken when she died. I loved her then; I love her now. And she is one of the reasons I believe. I wish I had taken her advice sooner.

Ione Hughes... During my early years on the streets I stayed with this remarkable lady and after joining the navy I visited her as often as I could while I was stationed at Great Lakes naval station. Ione loved God and she loved helping people. She helped many street people like me. If you recall she was the one involved with the incident when my wife 'lost' her voice. She walked and spoke with an air of authority that would intimidate most folks, but her love and kindness was so unlike what I was used to that I respected and adored her. She made a lasting impression on me and is one of my credible sources for what I believe.

Don wells….as previously mentioned, Don is the CRNA that invited me to church many years ago. To this day we are both surprised I accepted. God used Don to stop my fall into the abyss even though after a short reprieve I continued to the bottom. But throughout my journey to God Don has always encouraged me and lifted me up and prayed for me. Don, like me, probably considers himself to be a failure in many ways, but I see him as a mighty warrior in God's army. He has always stood strong in his faith and is unwavering in his devotion to Jesus. I can only hope to be seen as half the man he is in service to our Lord. I love him dearly as a brother in Christ and feel blessed to know we shall enjoy eternity together. Don is a man strong in his faith and is one of the many reasons I believe.

Joyce Meyer …. I do not personally know Joyce, but she was instrumental in my recovery and return to sanity. She had a troubled childhood like I did, and I felt like she understood broken people like me. God used her to help me via her teaching ministry. I have listened faithfully to her for years and every word is like God speaking directly to me. The wisdom of her teaching resonates loudly, and she is one of the many reasons I believe.

Jimmy Swaggart…. I have watched Jimmy for many years from his beginnings, to his fall, to his return. What I have learned from him is no matter how much we mess up, no matter how far we fall, no matter how deep in the mud we are, you need to get back up, face the cross, and press on no matter what. He is an incredible example of God's grace. Keeping our eyes on Jesus and ignoring the storm is the answer to all of life's problems and our failures. I thank God for Brother Swaggart and his ministry and is one of many reasons I believe.

Bill, Gary, Joe.... I attended Dayspring Baptist Church in Mobile, Alabama. Every Sunday I attend a small group for senior men. When I first started with this group there were about 8-12 each Sunday. Over the years several have left or died. It's now down to just the four of us. We discuss the sermon, our week, our struggles, and offer ourselves to help each other anytime needed. It's a wonderful thing to be able to sit with others like yourself and know that they have been on this journey of life a long time just like you and they truly understand where you are in life and what you are going through. These men have served God most of their lives through thick and thin and have remained faithful. We love Jesus. I am truly blessed to have these guys to lean on. They are my Godly support system and are one of many reasons I believe.

Johanna Portier… my gift from God. My wife truly loves the Lord. While we don't agree on absolutely everything spiritual, we are both on the same road going in the same direction. I respect her knowledge of the Bible, and the many hours she studies the Word. She is a faithful follower of Jesus and is one of many reasons I continue to believe.

These folks have impacted me spiritually as have others not listed, but there are two people who are not in this category that said something so profound that it impacted my life and changed my attitude about the way I deal with life and people. I will discuss them now.

Betty… I do not recall Betty's last name even though what she said to me is burned into my brain cells. She was a patient who was in her mid 30s and had MS. When I met her, she had been in a wheelchair for a couple of years.

Her body was twisted and shriveled up. She was literally skin and bones. She had had over 20 operations. She had a feeding tube, a colostomy, and a urine catheter. She was frail and talking was an effort. But... Betty had the biggest smile! And she was always happy! And she laughed all the time. After her last surgery she was put in the ICU overnight. I came in early the following morning to check on her. I was running a little late and was a bit annoyed over some personal issues. When I went into her room, I was greeted with a big smile so big it lit up the room! She said she was so glad to see me and wanted to know what I was frowning about. I didn't realize I was. I walked over to the side of her bed, stared at her for a few seconds and asked her if I could ask her a question. But first I had a comment. I said, Betty, look at me. I have good legs and arms, I am strong and healthy, I can run and jump, dance, drive a car and do a whole bunch of other things that you can't do. And my question to you is, why are you so dang happy and I'm not? Care to guess what she said???? She reached over and took my hand, looked straight into my eyes and said, "because you're crippled, and I'm not"!

    It was like a hot coal burning straight into my soul. I stared at her in stunned silence as I realized how right she was. She laughed and said for me not to take it so hard, I was going to be OK. I was amazed at the wisdom that came out of this wonderful woman. I was running late and needed to go so I thanked her for her honesty, and I would see her later. I left but didn't get to see her again because she was sent home. I spent several days pondering what she had told me. I now see most people as handicapped in some way and treat handicapped people like they are normal. I guess in some ways I still am a bit crippled, but I am so much better than I was thanks in no small way to Betty. I am sure she has passed by now, but I hope to see her again one day. I hope she knew how much she helped me.

Winston Churchill…. I think one of the reasons I have persevered in many bad situations is because of something this wise man said. I have read a lot about him on the internet and one story caught my interest and has served me well over the years. During WW2 the Germans were bombing England and had severely damaged London. Churchill called for a meeting with his generals and said they needed to do more to stop the bombing. The generals all agreed that things were bad but told Churchill they were doing their very best under the circumstances. Churchill said sometimes our best is not good enough, sometimes we must do what is required. Let that sink in for a while. I have incorporated this thought process into the way I solve problems. When faced with a difficult situation or issue, instead of 'doing my best' I decide what is required, and then do my best to get what is required done. Thank you, Winston Churchill.

Chapter 25

By now I have revealed enough about my life and experiences that you should be able to decide for yourself whether I am credible enough for you to believe that I have good reason to believe what I believe.

Or maybe I am just a brain damaged idiot who has had one too many drug feasts to have a normal functioning brain and truly needs to be ignored. Guess what? It's your choice.

God led you to this book. Ask yourself why. Are you already a born-again believer and just wanted to read about a fellow brother in Christ? If so, then I thank God for you and hope you have been encouraged and your faith strengthened. If not? If you do not have a relationship with your Creator, then why read this book? What is the need in your life that made you read my story? What part of my life is similar to yours? What are you looking for that you have not found yet?

Did you pick up this book hoping to see what it was that made me believe hoping you could find something to help you believe? If so, then my recommendation would be to try my God out for a while and see if He will work for you like He has for me... Talk to Him. He understands. He knows it's hard for some to believe. Tell Him you don't know if He is there or not, but you want to believe He is. Tell Him you want to know the truth about Jesus and if He was who He said He was. God looks upon the intent of your heart. If your intent is to know the truth and be set free, then be prepared for change. Let me tell you how to get started.

Tell God that you are not happy with your life, and you need a change. Tell Him you are a sinner, and you are repenting of your sins. Ask Him to forgive you. Tell Him you don't know how to live a better life and want His help. Tell Him you accept Jesus as your Lord and Savior and wish to follow Him from this day forward. If you do this and are sincere, you will be forgiven, and God will accept you as His child. It doesn't matter if you feel different or not. When you join the Army, you don't feel like a soldier immediately. You need to be with other soldiers and let them help and teach you how to be a good soldier. Find a Bible believing church and start reading your Bible.

I know it can be hard to know how to read your Bible so let me make some suggestions. Read the gospel of Luke and John to learn who Jesus is. Then read the book of Acts so you will know what is going on, and then read the book of Romans to learn God's plan of salvation. Once you know what's in these books you will have a better understanding of what to read next. Knowing what's in these four books will make reading and understanding the Bible easier. you can use King James, the amplified Bible or any of the versions written in current day English. It's the message of the gospel and reading about it that is more important than the version.

And very important, find a Christian friend you trust and can talk to about your journey. And like any new adventure you need to be committed and not give up no matter what. Be prepared for Satan to attack you and do all he can to discourage you. That is his job. Don't let him win! As you go on this journey with God you will notice changes in your life. A lot of people think they must clean themselves up and then present themselves to God. Not so!

You do not have to be a good soldier to join the army. You join and the army will make you into a good soldier. You need to just follow Him and He will clean you up, make repairs in your soul and begin to make Himself known to you just like He did for me. A verse in the Bible I live by is Proverbs 3, verse 5-6. It says to 'trust in the Lord with all your heart, to lean not into your own understanding, but acknowledge Him in all your ways and He will guide your path.' I have found this to be so very true in my life, and in the lives of many faithful Christians I know. YOU CAN DO THIS. And you too will begin to experience a wonderful Father, Lord, Savior, and Friend as I have. And then you will finally know and understand deep in your soul WHY I BELIEVE!

Epilogue

Whew! Can you believe the literary journey you and I have just gone on together? I sincerely hope I have conveyed something to you that helps you in some way. As I have said before this is not a complete autobiography, but rather a spiritual rags to riches story. I feel like God allowed my life to happen so I could write this book. Only an alcoholic can reach other alcoholics. Same with drug addicts. Same with parents who have lost a child, same with handicapped people, etc. They won't listen to anyone who doesn't understand their problem.

     I believe God allows certain things to happen to us so we can go out and save others with a similar problem. I see my life as a training program God put me through so I can help and encourage anyone I come in contact with. I understand child abuse, I understand drug and alcohol addiction, I understand failed relationships and divorce, I understand debt and financial loss, I understand the joy and pain in raising children, I understand deep depression that crushes your soul! I understand being lost and all alone, and I'm here to tell you that Jesus is the answer to all of these problems. If most folks who read my story think I am crazy, that is ok. If just one soul comes to know Jesus and His saving Grace by reading about my journey, then my life and all the pain and stupidity will have been worth it.

My final word for you is go in peace and may God richly bless you and yours now and forever, AMEN.

PS: Looking forward to seeing you in Heaven. I'll be down at the barn feeding the horses.

Made in the USA
Columbia, SC
16 November 2024